History of the Public Land Question in the United States

by Shosuke Sapporo Sato
(1856-1939)

with an introduction by Kerby Jackson

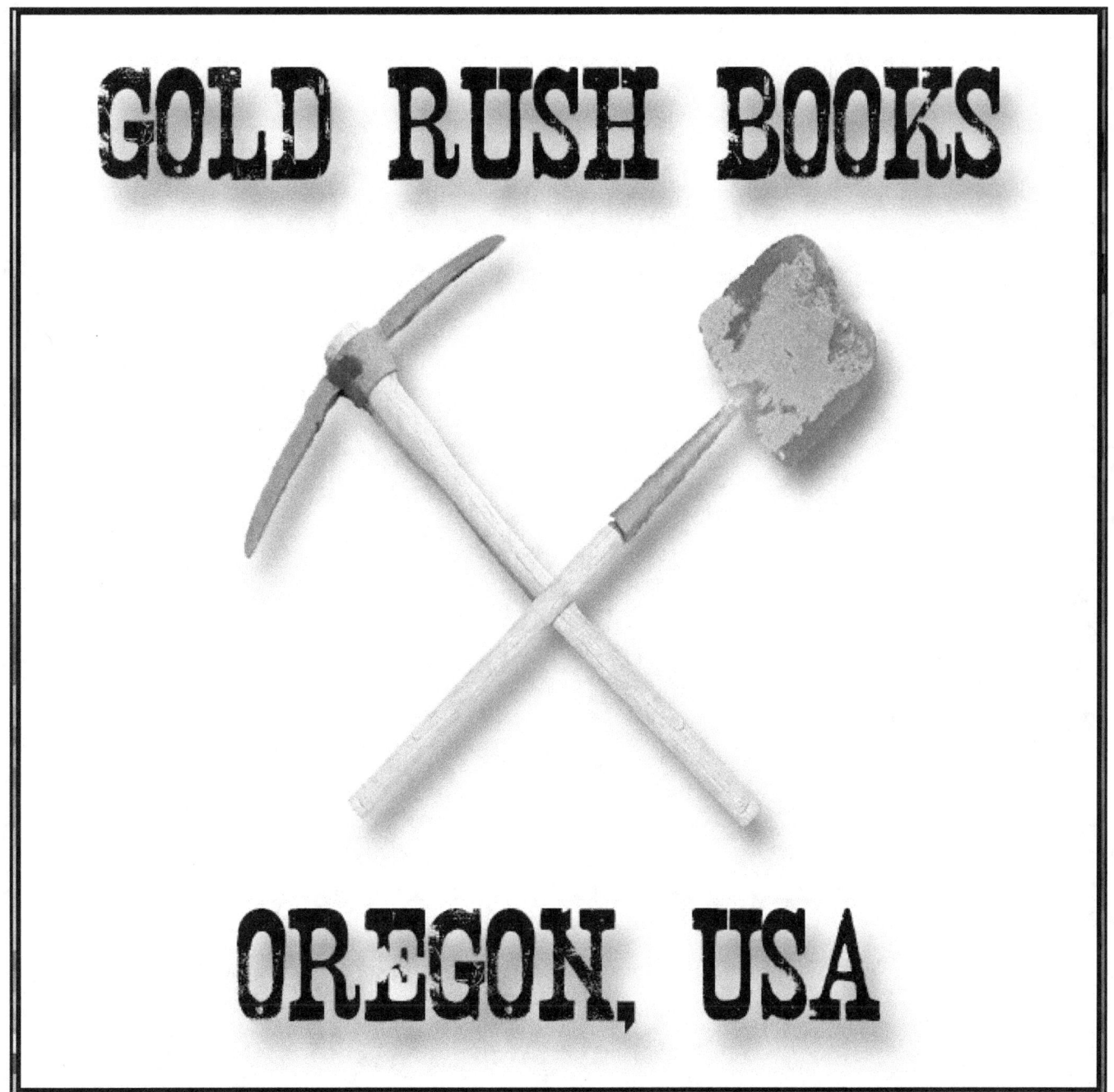

GOLD RUSH BOOKS

OREGON, USA

www.GoldMiningBooks.com

Introduction

It has often been said that *"gold is where you find it"*, but even beginning prospectors understand that their chances for finding something of value in the earth or in the streams of the Golden West are dramatically increased by going back to those places where gold and other minerals were once mined by our forerunners. Despite this, much of the contemporary information on local mining history that is currently available is mostly a result of mere local folklore and persistent rumors of major strikes, the details and facts of which, have long been distorted. Long gone are the old timers and with them, the days of first hand knowledge of the mines of the area and how they operated. Also long gone are most of their notes, their assay reports, their mine maps and personal scrapbooks, along with most of the surveys and reports that were performed for them by private and government geologists. Even published books such as this one are often retired to the local landfill or backyard burn pile by the descendents of those old timers and disappear at an alarming rate. Despite the fact that we live in the so-called "Information Age" where information is supposedly only the push of a button on a keyboard away, true insight into mining properties remains illusive and hard to come by, even to those of us who seek out this sort of information as if our lives depend upon it. Without this type of information readily available to the average independent miner, there is little hope that our metal mining industry will ever recover.

This important volume and others like it, are being presented in their entirety again, in the hope that the average prospector will no longer stumble through the overgrown hills and the tailing strewn creeks without being well informed enough to have a chance to succeed at his ventures.

Kerby Jackson
Josephine County, Oregon
May 2018

PREFACE.

This work was undertaken in pursuance of special instructions from the Japanese Government to investigate certain questions of agrarian and economic interest in the United States. In presenting one part of my work to the public, I desire to express my special gratitude to Dr. H. B. Adams, of the Johns Hopkins University, to whose constant encouragement and kind guidance I greatly owe the completion of the present monograph.

Since the author began to write this paper in the autumn of 1884, the Land Question has steadily advanced to a foremost place among the reform measures of the national administration. Especially within the past year has it attracted marked attention. Politicians and the public press are both interested in the land question. For several years the Labor press has been agitating it.* The *North American Review* took up the subject of Landholding in the United States, in a series of articles beginning in January, 1886. The *New York Herald* recently attacked many current abuses in land entries, and informed the American public of the methods by which unscrupulous land-grabbers steal the public lands. Works of high merit on the subject of the land question have been published. The Report of Commissioner Sparks for 1885 is most valuable. The Commissioner treats the land question with an ardent spirit of reform. He is fully aware of the importance of his subject. Mr. Phillips, in his "Labor, Land, and Law" (Scribners, 1886), is also a valuable contributor to the literature of the land question. That even the common people in America are now conscious of the grave abuses in the agrarian administration of the United States and demand a

---

* It is a highly significant fact that the Homestead laws and recent agitation of the Land Question are the outgrowth of the American labor movement, beginning about the year 1825 with the formation of the Workingmen's Party. The chief agrarian demands of that party subsequently became laws of the land. The agrarian problems of the American people have historical parallels not only in the agrarian history of republican Rome, but in the economic history of Germany, England, and Ireland. The land question in Germany, left unsettled by the Reformation and the Peasant Wars, found its final solution in the reforms of Baron vom Stein and his successors. In England the land question is still unsolved, notwithstanding the Irish Land Acts, which are the most radical agrarian laws of modern times.—ED.

reform, is shown by the action recently taken by the Knights of Labor in their convention at Cleveland, Ohio. In their platform the Knights adopted resolutions touching land reform, and, as a sign of the times, I here insert the text:

"(1) We demand that the public lands be reserved for actual settlers only. (2) We demand that all lands owned by individuals or corporations in excess of 160 acres not under cultivation shall be taxed to their full value, the same as cultivated lands. (3) We demand the immediate forfeiture of all lands where the conditions of the grants have not been complied with. (4) We demand that patents be at once issued for all lands where the conditions have been complied with, and that taxes be assessed on these lands as if under cultivation. (5) We demand the immediate removal of all fences from the public lands. (6) We demand that after 1890 the Government obtain possession by purchase of all lands now held by aliens at appraised valuations. (7) We demand that after 1886 aliens be prohibited from obtaining land titles."

These demands seem to me neither extreme nor radical. On the contrary, they are simply an echo of popular sentiment. Some of the demands by the Knights were already under the consideration of Congress. The Senate passed bills on the 1st and 3d of June, 1886, providing for the restriction of alien ownership of land and taxing railroad land grants. On the 2d of June the Secretary of the Interior ordered the suspension of entries under "pre-emption, timber culture and desert land" till the 1st of August, 1886. This order was in view of the consideration in Congress of the removal of these useless and much abused land laws from the statutes of the United States. "The question of land reform like the world does move," says a *Herald* correspondent. It will "move" until the Homestead Act becomes the only settlement law of the country, and the public lands are restored to the Government for the use of actual settlers.

BALTIMORE, MD., *June* 14, 1886.

CONTENTS.

Contents.

Contents.

HISTORY OF THE LAND QUESTION IN THE UNITED STATES.

INTRODUCTION.

ORIGIN AND IMPORTANCE OF THE PUBLIC DOMAIN.

The War of Independence severed political connections between the English colonies and their mother country. The colonies became States, and the States assumed a sovereign power. The thirteen colonies which were planted in the region along the Atlantic border formed the American Union; and its territory, as recognized in the treaty of 1783, extended from the Atlantic on the east to the Mississippi in the west, and from the Great Lakes in the north to the Gulf of Mexico in the south. This constituted the national domain of the United States, and embraced an area of about 830,000 square miles. That portion of the national domain lying immediately west of the Alleghany mountains and northwest of the Ohio river was claimed by several States, but was ceded by them to the National Government after a long-protracted controversy. Likewise the region southeast of the Ohio was ceded to the Government by the then three southernmost States. These lands formed a nucleus of the public domain of the United States, and contained an area of about 404,000 square miles. Out of this public domain arose several republican commonwealths, which added much to the strength and wealth of the Union.

The creation of the public domain forms an important epoch in the history of American Politics. Its subsequent expansion; the mode of its administration; legislation for its government; its relation to constitutional questions; the diplomacy and politics involved in its acquisition; its international boundary questions; the enactment of settlement laws; the attraction of immigrants and growth of population; internal improvements and increased facilities of transportation; the discovery of precious metals, and other similar topics of interest might be cited here in connection with the public domain. They afford to the student of politics and economics an ample field of study and investigation, and show in a measure what important relations the public domain has had with the affairs of the nation and what vital questions have been involved in it.

Perhaps slavery and the public domain are the two most important factors in the politico-economic history of the United States. In this country slavery has had a beginning and an end. Its beginning may be traced back to colonial times—to the introduction of negroes into Virginia in 1619. This peculiar institution, after an existence of nearly two centuries and a half, has finally met with its fate. The reconstruction of society upon a true economic basis is the chief work of to-day in the sections of the country where slavery once prevailed. Slavery may well be forgotten by the younger generation. It already belongs to the province of "past politics." But the public domain has its actual life in present history. Bills have been pending in the National Legislature which aim to repeal certain out-lived settlement laws. The question of a forfeiture of a Railroad Land Grant has just been decided against a railroad corporation for its non-fulfilment of conditions. The Senate has two standing committees on the Public Lands, and the House of Representatives one committee on the same, while the General Land Office is one of the most important branches in the civil service of the Government. The concentration of landed property into the hands of foreign capitalists, which means the introduction of British Absenteeism, has been drawing attention from the public and the press. Fraudulent entries and adventurous trespass on the public lands called forth sharp words from Mr. Cleveland in his inaugural address, to the effect that "care for the property of the nation and for the needs of future settlers requires that the public domain should be protected from purloining schemes and unlawful occupation." Again, justice demands the protection of the Indians in their right of occupancy from the lawlessness of so-called "boomers." In this and all other questions, the public interest is deeply concerned with the administration and disposition of the public domain. Notwithstanding the rapid disposition of public lands, there yet remain scattered all over the southern, the western, and the Pacific regions, vast tracts of unoccupied lands, the aggregate area of which is almost twice as great as that of the national domain in 1783. Tides of immigration still flow from across the ocean. Millions of homes can be created. An immense wealth and vast resources can be developed. Towns will multiply; counties will grow; free institutions will spring into life. This material advance and prosperity will be due to the public domain and its judicious disposition. Homestead laws will continue to build up the Great West in the future as they have done in the past. The importance of the public domain, however, seems to have been rarely and but recently emphasized by the student of American history.

FUTURE OF THE PUBLIC DOMAIN.

The public domain will continue to exist till all the unoccupied lands are disposed of. That time, however, is remote. This generation will not see the public domain fully exhausted. Texas may not be the last annexation, and Alaska may not be the last purchase. The drift of political affairs may yet cause the union of two kindred nationalities in a republican bond under a federal government. Free social and commercial intercourse may anglicize Latin neighbors on the main-land of America as well as on adjacent islands, and precipitate a treaty of purchase or annexation.   During the period of ninety years the national domain has grown almost five times as great as its original extent.   Its future expansion may not be altogether a matter of political imagination.

The growth of territory has been accompanied by the growth of population and the rise of commonwealths.   The public domain makes a home for the poor and the oppressed of over-populated European countries.   The first immigration census, taken in 1820, shows the insignificant number of 8,385.   In 1883 the census shows an influx of foreign population amounting to nearly six hundred thousand people.   In sixty-three years Europe contributed to the population of the United States more than twelve millions of people.   The West is a paradise for the settler.   Public land is free of cost to every one who comes in good faith.   Broad acres await labor and industry, cultivation and improvement.   Mother Nature is lavish in her gifts.   The virgin soil yields profitable returns.   The thrifty yeomanry, inspired with the spirit of free institutions, build up local and municipal governments.   Every naturalized citizen enjoys political rights, and feels perfectly at home, though in a strange land.   Democratic-republican principles permeate local, municipal, and State institutions.

These self-governing institutions and republican common-wealths are really a monument to the memory of early legislators and statesmen, who brought that complicated question of land-cessions to a successful issue, who framed a republican consti-tution for the government of the Western Territory, and achieved the profitable purchase of a vast empire beyond the Mississippi, thus laying foundations for a nation's wealth and prosperity.   The growth and development of the United States in size, wealth, resources, and population not only show the progressive power of modern civilization, but also testify to an historical truth, that the movement of Indo-European popu-lation has been in a westerly direction ever since its first historical emigration from the heart of Asia.   The acquisition of a great national domain in the West has attracted to the

United States the people of various Indo-European stocks.
To vast primeval forests and broad plains have come Germanic, Latin, and Scandinavian nationalities, who are fast being assimilated with an Anglo-American nationality in a new world. However widely local institutions and customs may vary, however much birth and nationality may differ, there yet prevails a unique *American* nationality, which is ever augmenting and ever increasing in wealth and prosperity. The statesmen who first made laws regulating the public domain could no more have foreseen the rise of such a great republic than the early planters of Virginia or hardy Puritan settlers of Massachusetts could have foreseen the independence of their children's children.

PUBLIC LAND POLICY OF THE UNITED STATES.

The territorial expansion of the United States has by no means always been the result of an aggressive policy. The country maintains a traditional peace policy in all its foreign relations. Circumstances have led the nation to acquire territories which, both geographically and politically, were best fitted to become members of the American Union. The imperial ambition of Napoleon to rule Europe caused him to part with the French province of Louisiana in America. The down-trodden powers in the Old World finally regained their freedom and recovered their territories after years of bloody struggle; but, on this side of the Atlantic, the foresight of Mr. Jefferson and the diplomacy of his colleagues secured to the United States its most important possession beyond the Mississippi, one year before the Corsican general assumed the crown of Charlemagne. The purchase of Florida from Spain in 1819 forever settled a boundary dispute in West Florida, and consolidated a national interest in the development of resources by the United States in their south-eastern territories. The two rival powers of old colonial times, Spain and France, thus lost a permanent hold of their colonies in America, and this country was no longer to be considered as subject to colonization by any European power. Time had changed the affairs of nations, and the "Monroe Doctrine" succeeded the right of discovery and exploration in the New World. Unoccupied lands were no longer spoils of grasping adventurers under a foreign flag, but became an American domain, subject to the settlement laws of a free and independent republic.

AGRARIAN LAWS OF ROME AND THE UNITED STATES.

History tells us of the evolution of landed property from communal to private ownership, and from equal to unequal divisions. "The Roman idea of a right of absolute property," says Laveleye,[1] "was always foreign to Greece. The territory of the State was regarded as belonging to it alone." The distribution of public land taxed the wisdom of Greek lawgivers, and its concentration into the hands of a few was often a cause of political revolution. It is in the famous Licinian laws of the Roman Republic that we find a germ of modern public-land laws. First of all, the Lex Licinia[2] required the ager publicus to be defined. Then, if there was any encroachment, it had to be surrendered to the State. Such survey of public lands and such prevention of unlawful occupation have been among the first requisites in the administration of the public domain in modern times. Secondly, by the Licinian law, every estate in the public lands, which was required to be of a lawful size, with peaceful occupation, was declared by the State to be good against third parties. This was virtually the same as the modern right of pre-emption, which is secured to every honest settler. Thirdly, every Roman citizen had a right to occupy public lands in conformity to the laws. To the Romans, citizenship was a necessary qualification to the enjoyment of privileges in the public lands.

---

[1] Laveleye's Primitive Property, 158.
[2] Niebuhr, Römische Geschichte, Vol. III, 14–17.

So it is to-day in the United States. Pre-emption right and homestead-entry are allowed to aliens only on the condition that they will become citizens of the United States. Fourthly, the Licinian law forbade any person to possess more than 500 jugera, or about 350 acres of public land, and to pasture more than a hundred head of large cattle or five hundred head of small cattle on the same. The spirit of settlement laws in the United States seems to be inclining toward parcelling out public lands into small holdings. One hundred and sixty acres of land is a maximum quantity allowed to a homesteader, although any settler can obtain 1,120 acres of public land under the existing settlement laws.[1]

Laboulaye[2] says that "The law of the five hundred jugera is always quoted by them [referring to Varro, Pliny and Columella] with admiration, as being the first which recognized the evil, and sought to remedy it by retarding the formation of those vast domains or *latifundia* which depopulated Italy, and after Italy, the whole empire." The Homestead Act, which is spoken of as the outgrowth of "the concentrated wisdom of legislation for settlement of the public lands,"[3] would undoubtedly increase the number of free proprietors and build up local communities in the United States, as the law of five hundred jugera would have done for the ancient republic. The just and equal distribution of public lands is the spirit of both laws. As to the limitation of the number of head of cattle to be pastured on public lands we have a similar fact in the local agrarian history of New England towns. At Salem[4] the pasturage on every ten acres of common fields was limited to 6 cows, 4 oxen, 3 horses, or 12 yearlings or 24 calves. Whether it is in small local communities or in extensive terri-

---

[1] The Public Domain, 1159.

[2] Quoted by Laveleye in Primitive Property, 167.

[3] The Public Domain, 350.

[4] H. B. Adams. "Village Communities of Cape Ann and Salem." Johns Hopkins Univ. Studies in Historical and Political Science. First Series, IX–X.

tories, agrarian interests are the same, and men are everywhere inclined to demand an equal share in agrarian benefits.   As to the rest of the Licinian law, Niebuhr states that the occupants of public lands were required to offer to the State a certain part of the produce of the soil, and that the State defrayed the expense of the army with the income thus derived.

GERMAN, ENGLISH, AND AMERICAN FOLK LAND.

The Germanic common mark and the Anglo-Saxon focland[1] correspond to the Roman ager publicus, and the present public domain of the United States is held upon essentially the same principles as the mark, focland, and ager publicus. Just as the arable mark, or the mark of the township, was parcelled out to individuals from the common mark among the ancient Germans, or as bocland was registered focland among the Anglo-Saxons, so the homestead is granted to the American settler out of the public domain.   The homestead so granted is allodial and held in fee-simple.   Allodial ownership and fee-simple tenure were essential features of ancient Teutonic institutions, and here we find the wholesome influence and effect of a free agrarian system of Germanic origin upon the focland of the American people.

We have already seen in the old Licinian laws some parallel with the American settlement laws, either in spirit or in principle.   This comparative study has also led us to recognize the fact that the Germanic allodial land system has been reproduced in the method of parcelling out free, independent homesteads from the public domain.   But we must bear in mind the true historical connection between American and Germanic agrarian institutions.   American settlers first introduced mild forms of English feudal tenure, but these were transformed in course of time into allodial tenure.   In fact, the American agrarian system has no direct connection with

---

[1] **Systems of Land Tenure.** Cobden Club Edition, 286.

the old Germanic customs in the "Gemeinde," any more than it has with the customs of the Russian *Mir* or Swiss *Allmends.*

The English common law is to-day the law of all the States of the American Union with the exception of one State, viz. Louisiana. English feudal land laws were the direct source and origin of early American land tenure, and even to-day they still govern more or less the transfer of landed property in some of the older States.

After the Revolution, most States abolished all feudal incidents connected with landed property. For instance, "By the statute of February 20, 1787, New York abolished all military tenures, transferring them into free and common socage, and making all State grants entirely allodial. The revised statutes, going into effect in 1830, abolished the last shadow of feudal tenure, and made allodial proprietorship the sole title to private land, and this property liable to forfeiture only by escheat."[1] In spite of the simplified method of bargain and sale, the conveyance of real estate, however, seems to retain some feudal incidents which are complained of as cumbersome and as involving needless expenses.

A leading New York journal[2] commented on this subject in its editorial columns as follows: "By the Constitution of the State of New York, 'all feudal tenures of every description, with all their incidents, are declared to be abolished,' but as a matter of fact the incidents of feudal tenure are not all abolished. This very cumbrousness and complexity of the transfer of land is one of them, and the right of dower is distinctly another. The common law of England upon the subject of real property is a survival from feudal times, and it has nowhere in this country been completely remodeled in conformity with the needs and usages of an industrial community. There is, by law, a special sanctity attached to ownership of

---

[1] Quoted in Public Domain, 159, from Mr. Wilson's Report of the General Land Office.

[2] New York Times, December 30, 1884.

land as compared with that of other property, and the alienation of it is purposely made difficult.   In England, this treatment of land still corresponds to a real public sentiment.   The owner of land is an object of much more social consideration than the owner of an equal value in personal property.   Inasmuch as the 'landed interest' still governs Great Britain, it is to be expected that British laws should make as troublesome as possible the acquisition of 'estates' by new men who have enriched themselves and who aspire to 'found families.' We have abolished primogeniture and entail, which are the chief legal supports of the landed aristocracy.   But we have by no means got rid in our laws of the feudal habit of regarding property in land as more important to the State than other property, and it is from this habit that the practice of making land less easily alienable than other property proceeds."

FEUDAL LAND LAWS OF ENGLAND.

The landed interests are everywhere decidedly conservative, and land laws are made to suit the conservative elements of the nation.   The interest of a landed aristocracy is nowhere better protected than in England by a complicated land system. The land system of England is feudal, and its structure very complex and heterogeneous.   "The main body of the technical expressions of the law, and of the technical habit of thought," says Mr. Pollock in his Land Laws, "is derived from feudalism. . . . .   So great is the technical complication and difficulty of our laws on the subject, that within the special studies of the legal profession the study of them is a specialty of itself."[1]

Feudalism was in full operation in England when Jamestown was planted by the Virginia Company in 1607.   Feudal land tenures and customs were then still practically binding on landed property.   Estates were fettered by entail and inherit-

---

[1] The Land Laws, by Frederick Pollock, 2-3.

ance, limited to primogeniture or ultimogeniture. Tenures were still in knight service. The abolition of military tenures in England took place half a century later than the settlement in Jamestown. It was done by the 12th, Charles II., cap. 24, in 1660.[1] By this act, "all freehold tenures were reduced to the one type of free and common socage, with an important twofold result. First, all the vexatious incidents of military tenure disappeared with the tenure itself; only ancient money rents might remain payable by the tenant, which had already become, by the changes in the value of money since they were fixed, almost or altogether nominal. Next, inasmuch as the statute of 1540 had enabled tenants in fee-simple to dispose by will of the whole of their socage lands, and socage was now made the only freehold tenure, the whole of the fee-simple land in the kingdom became disposable by will. Feudal tenancy was converted for all practical purposes into full ownership."

For fully six centuries military tenures shaped the history of land laws in England. As the Norman Conquest and Domesday Book made a transition from the Anglo-Saxon allodial land system into the feudal land system, so the abolition of military tenures by Charles II. was a transition from the feudal land system to a more liberal land system of a testamental succession and free alienation, but not by any means a return to the ancient Anglo-Saxon land laws in theory or in practice. The English land laws may be called Reformed Feudal Land Laws. They retain the essential feature of feudalism, and that is the reason why they are so complex and so confusing.

LAND TENURE IN COLONIAL TIMES.

Notwithstanding the prevailing feudal land laws in England during the seventeenth century, the English colonists in

---

[1] Landholding in England, by Joseph Fisher, Humboldt Library, 36 ; or Pollock's Land Laws, 125.

America were fortunate enough to secure a milder form of land tenure from the British Crown. The charter granted to Sir Walter Raleigh in 1584 specified that lands were to be held in fee-simple. All the rest of royal charters, beginning with the charter to the Virginia Company in 1606 and ending with that granted to the Trustees of Georgia in 1732, granted lands in free and common socage, that is, in free tenure without military service. The source of all land titles was in the Crown. The King was the Lord Paramount of all the lands held by the colonists. By virtue of discovery, conquest, colonization, and the acknowledged principle of feudalism, the British Crown was the only legal source of ownership of landed property by the English colonists. Sometimes a recognition of fealty was required; sometimes quit-rent was exacted by the Crown. Feudal incidents were unavoidably brought to the colonies. Proprietorship in the middle colonies, and aristocracy in the southern colonies, showed that mediæval institutions were planted in some measure upon the virgin soil of America. Within the colony of New Netherlands, afterwards New York, a small feudal principality, with almost an independent sovereign power, was erected by Patroon Rensselaer. The essential features of this great proprietary survived long after the Revolution.[1]

In theory, titles derived from the Crown were complete and unconditioned so far as the colonists themselves were concerned; but in practice they were far from being so. The right of the aborigines was to be respected by the settlers. Indians were allowed right of occupancy. The Crown had the titular right, but the Indians a possessory right. The grant of lands by the Crown was of no use unless the savages turned them over to settlers. There were two ways opened to the settlers, either of which would secure to them full ownership of lands. The one was by the use of force; the

---

[1] Mrs. Martha J. Lamb, "The Van Rensselaer Manor," in Magazine of American History, January, 1884.

other by purchase. Humane and Christian principles alike forbade the use of force, although the colonists often violated both. The colonies secured the right of pre-emption in most cases. Negotiation with and purchase from the original possessors finally made the colonists realize the full possession of lands which their titular lord so lavishly granted them. Not only did royal grants conflict with the Indian rights, but they conflicted with themselves. Overlapping grants occasioned many legal disputes about boundaries, *e. g.* in the case of Maryland and Pennsylvania.[1] In the case of Virginia and Maryland such disputes actually resulted in colonial war. Again, the international territorial conflicts of the principal colonizing powers were among the chief events in the colonial history of America. The Treaty of Paris in 1763 made England the dominant power in the regions along the Atlantic border and east of the Mississippi river. Twenty years afterwards, however, England had to sign another treaty, Versailles, 1783, and acknowledge the independence of the United States. The Crown lands created by the royal proclamation of 1763 were destined to become the public domain of a great republic.

LAND TENURE AFTER THE REVOLUTION.

The revolution for political freedom brought a revolution in the agrarian laws of the country. The United States became, within limits, a successor to the British Crown, and a source of land titles. The public domain created after the Revolution became the public property of a new nation instead of a titular sovereign. It was now held in trust by the national government of the United States, to dispose of in the best interest of the whole people. Feudal incidents were now abolished. By the Ordinance of 1787, absolute ownership of

---

[1] Cf. W. B. Scaife on the Boundary Disputes between Pennsylvania and Maryland, in the Pennsylvania Magazine of History and Biography, October, 1885.

land was guaranteed. There was to be no more primogeniture nor entail on the public domain. Certainly land, the most essential element in the production of economic goods, everywhere deserves the most enlightened and liberal policy which statesmen can conceive. It should subserve the cause of the greatest production and the best interests of the whole people. The liberal land policy devised by the government of the United States has been followed by other nations. France, in the Revolution of 1789; Prussia, in the legislation of 1811; Russia, in the Emancipation Act of 1861, and, finally, Japan in the abolition of feudalism in 1871,—all these nations took a great step forward. They removed slavish and cumbrous restrictions which had rested upon landed property. Free alienation, testamentary disposition, and just inheritance should characterize liberal agrarian laws. These were secured not only for the public domain of the United States, but also for the older individual States themselves.

Speaking of the ownership of the land in America, Mr. Cunningham, an English writer,[1] some years ago, in his "Social Well-Being," says : " In the United States there are no land laws established by which the soil is made to fall gradually into the hands of a few great families, as in Great Britain. There are generally no restrictions upon its sale, its inheritance, or its application. The system of occupation is generally that of small proprietors.[2] The idea which pervades the whole American people is that of the advisability of universal proprietorship, and the feeling against anything approaching to landlordism is pronounced." More recent investigators say that the tenant farms are increasing in an alarming ratio in the United States, especially in the Northwestern States. A fear is also expressed that the growth of American *latifundia* will bring ominous effects upon the na-

---

[1] Conditions of Social Well-Being, 173.

[2] For the controversy on the size of farms in the United States between General Walker and Mr. George, see Henry George's Social Problems, pp. 333–356.

tional economy of the American people.   Whether these views are substantiated by facts or not, is now an open question.[1]

It was the Revolution that created the public domain of the United States, and it was the public domain that made necessary a liberal agrarian system.   Not only did the public domain call forth land laws that were subversive of feudal incidents, but it became instrumental in establishing the Union upon the basis of a common economic interest.   In the possession of public lands the old States found a common tie which bound them permanently together.   However widely political ideas might differ, however much economic interests might antagonize sections, however greatly social institutions and customs might vary, there remained, back of the Alleghany mountains, a vast tract of focland, in the settlement and disposition of which all the States found a common interest. That interest bound together the sovereign States into a territorial commonwealth.[2]   The public lands were the backbone of the United States.   The history of their constitutional development cannot be understood without a study of the land question.

Congress under the Articles of Confederation was an impotent organ.   It never discharged the purpose for which it was created.   That body, however, did one thing of great merit. It legislated on the government of the Northwestern Territory. It passed the Ordinance of 1787.   This was a masterly work of genuine statesmanship.   It was the Bill of Rights for the future settler of the Public Domain.   It was the American Magna Charta.   Under this ordinance territories prospered and commonwealths arose.

RELATIONS OF THE PUBLIC DOMAIN TO NATIONAL LIFE.

We have seen that the institution of the public domain gave a fatal stroke to feudal land tenures; it bound the Union

---

[1] See a series of articles in the North American Review, January, 1886, and succeeding numbers.

[2] See H. B. Adams.   University Studies.   Third Series, I.

together by an economic bond, and called forth the Ordinance of 1787. We shall now briefly consider what important ends the public domain has served in the politico-economic history of the United States.

1. Public lands were used as bounties to veteran soldiers and sailors, from the time of the Revolution down to the late Civil War.

2. Public lands were once an important source of public revenue, and formed a basis for national finance.

3. Public lands and diplomacy have often been related in the affairs of the nation. The purchase of territories from the foreign powers and the negotiation about boundary disputes called forth the diplomacy of Livingston, Pinckney, Monroe, and other statesmen.

4. The survey and administration of public lands were initiated by the two most eminent statesmen, Jefferson and Hamilton. Mr. Jefferson, as chairman of a committee in the Congress of 1784, furnished the basis of the present system of survey known as the "rectangular system," and Hamilton, as Secretary of Treasury, furnished the basis of the present method of administration in 1790.

5. Public lands have been the means of effecting internal improvements. Canals, highways, and levees have been constructed under the stimulus of public land grants.

6. The promotion of education in the United States is closely connected with public lands. The Ordinance of 1787 recognized the importance of education. Public land grants for mechanical and agricultural institutions, as well as for State universities and public schools, have aided in their foundation and maintenance.

7. Public lands have had great influence upon the problem of transportation. If it were not for public lands, the railroads which now form the great highways of the nation—for example, the Central Pacific and Union Pacific—could not have been built so soon. Grave abuses there may have been, but the benefits resulting from the facility of transportation cannot be gainsaid.

8. The mineral resources of the public lands form an important part of America's national wealth. The discovery of gold in California marks an epoch in the world's economy. Mining laws are, therefore, of a great consequence to the nation.

9. Foreign landlordism, private claims, and land litigations are all connected more or less with the public lands.

10. Lastly, the relation of public lands to immigration suggests an important economic problem. "No State without people" should be the political maxim of statesmen in encouraging foreign immigration. Free homes and free institutions, free labor and free soil, are the best capital for the development of the resources of the Great West.

Such is the scope of the land question in the general economy of the United States. The origin of the public domain, its subsequent expansion, the history of its administration, the various land grants, and the chief features of settlement laws, will be the subjects of special investigation in the following chapters.

I.

FORMATION OF THE PUBLIC DOMAIN.

The public domain of the United States was acquired through cession, purchase, and conquest. Its acquisition had been precipitated by a combination of varied political and economical considerations. The desire of firm union and the safety of the whole confederacy peacefully terminated the disputed claims of the larger States to the western lands. The prospect of fishery and the development of natural resources must have prompted the action of President Johnson's administration in the purchase of Alaska. The first acquisition of public land took place on March 1, 1781, and the last acquisition on March 30, 1867. Between these two periods there were several acquisitions of territory, whose history will be treated in its proper place. The first subject that should engage our attention is the

CESSIONS BY THE STATES.[1]

From a territorial point of view, the State cessions may be divided into two classes: the first embraces the territory northwest of the Ohio river, and the second covers the territory southeast of the Ohio.   Twenty-one years intervened between the first and last State cession.   New York was the first State that surrendered her claim to the northwestern territory, while Georgia was the last one that parted with her claim, by which the State cessions were made complete.

CLAIMANTS TO THE "CROWN LANDS."

It was the northwestern territory, or the "Crown Lands," that occasioned the greatest discussion in Congress.   The territory was claimed by several States.   The claimants were Massachusetts, Virginia, Connecticut, and New York.

Massachusetts based her claims upon the charter granted to her by William and Mary in 1691.[2]   She claimed that portion of the northwestern territory which was bounded on the west by the Mississippi river, on the south by about forty-two degrees of north latitude, and on the north and east by Lakes Superior and Huron, respectively.   The territory now lies in the States of Wisconsin and Michigan, partly in the eastern part of Minnesota, and partly in the northern part of Illinois.   It embraces an area of 54,000 square miles.   This territory was also disputed and claimed by Virginia.

The claim of Virginia was a most extended one.   Under the charter granted by James I. in 1609,[3] she claimed the entire territory west of Pennsylvania, and northwest of the

---

[1] See for the State cessions, Dr. H. B. Adams' Maryland's Influence upon Land Cessions to the United States, in J. H. U. Studies, 3d Series, No. 1.

[2] Laws of the United States (Duane Edition), Vol. I, 462.

[3] Laws of the United States (Duane Edition), Vol. I, 465.   Hening's Statutes, Vol. IX, 118.

Ohio river, and below the forty-first parallel of north latitude. She also claimed the territory lying south of the Ohio river, and north of her southern boundary, a territory now in the State of Kentucky.   Another claim which Virginia set forth by reason of conquest and occupancy, was to the territory extending northward from the forty-first degree of north latitude, toward the Lakes, which claim was disputed both by Massachusetts and Connecticut.   The claim of Virginia, excluding Kentucky, embraced an area of 265,562 square miles.

The claim of Connecticut, like that of Massachusetts, was an extension of her northern and southern boundary lines, under the charter granted by the British Crown.   They began with the western boundaries of New York and Pennsylvania, and extended as far west as the Mississippi.[1]   The territory now lies in the south of the State of Michigan, and in the north of the States of Ohio, Indiana, and Illinois.   Its area was estimated at 40,000 square miles.

'New York based her claim to the western lands chiefly upon various treaties which she made with the Six Nations and their tributaries, by which she acquired jurisdiction over their entire western territory.[2]   The territory of the Indian nations which New York claimed was indefinite in area, but was situated west of Pennsylvania and north of the Ohio river. *l*

Such were the conflicting claims of the four principal States of the Union over the western lands north of the Ohio river. South of it, the Carolinas and Georgia had their respective claims to an extension of their western boundaries.   The rest of the Union, New Hampshire, Rhode Island, New Jersey, Delaware, Pennsylvania, and Maryland, had definite boundary lines by the time the Revolutionary war broke out. Pennsylvania had a controversy with Connecticut, which was

---

[1] Laws of the United States (Duane Edition), Vol. I, 464.
[2] Journals of Congress, Vol. IV, 21.

known as the " Wyoming Controversy." It related to the jurisdiction over certain lands lying in the northern part of Pennsylvania, but this controversy was decided in 1782 in favor of Pennsylvania by a Federal Court, to which the question was referred according to the provision in the ninth article of the Confederation.[1]

WESTERN TERRITORY BEFORE THE REVOLUTION.

Claims to western territory by the several large States began with the Revolution. Prior to the Revolution, the colonies had no legal claim to jurisdiction over the western lands, which were set apart from the colonial territories as the " Crown Lands," by the royal proclamation of 1763.[2] The British Crown divided the territory which it acquired from France and Spain by the treaty of Paris in 1763, into four provinces: Quebec, East Florida, West Florida, and Grenada. All the lands which were not included within these provinces, nor within the grant to the Hudson Bay Company, were reserved for the use of the Indians. The colonies were forbidden to make purchase or settlement of any of these reserved lands without first obtaining royal permission. These lands were the so-called " Crown Lands."

The fertility and resources of these western lands seemed, from early times, to have attracted adventurous settlers. In 1748 the Ohio Company was formed, and in the following year secured 600,000 acres of land on the Ohio river.[3] The royal grant stipulated that the company should be free from quit-rent for ten years, provided in seven years there were one hundred families, and they had built a fort sufficient to protect the settlement. On June 12, 1749, the Loyal Company was organized and obtained the grant for 800,000 acres of

---

[1] Journals of Congress, IV, 129.

[2] Laws of the United States (Duane Edition), Vol. I, 443.

[3] Holmes' Annals of America, Vol. II, 39.

land.[1] On October 29, 1757, another land company, known as Greenbriar Company, was started and obtained the grant for 100,000 acres of land.[2]

After the treaty of Paris, by which the British Crown became the sole owner of the western territory, several land companies were organized with the view of making settlements back of the original colonies. In 1766 the Walpole Company was proposed. In 1769 the company petitioned for a grant of two and a half millions of the western lands, between 38° and 42° north latitude and east of the Scioto river. On August 14, 1772, the petition was finally granted by the Crown.[3] In 1769 the Mississippi Company[4] was started by some of the prominent Virginians as a rival to the Walpole Company. In North Carolina the Transylvania Company was organized in 1775.[5]

Both before and after the treaty of Paris these land companies petitioned directly to the British Crown for the grant of lands, and not to any colonial government. The Crown assumed the jurisdiction over the western lands, and the provincial governors had the power to issue land warrants to such persons only as were awarded lands by the Crown for services in the French and Indian war.

REVOLUTION AND THE LAND CONTROVERSY.

When the Revolutionary War broke out and the Articles of the Confederation were submitted for ratification to the Legislatures of the States, the question of the western lands became a momentous problem in the politics of the Confederacy. Virginia, Massachusetts, Connecticut, New York, the Carolinas, and Georgia treated the royal proclamation of 1763 as a nullity, and claimed an extension of their western boundary lines under their old charters; while the rest of the members of the Union protested against the claims of the

---

[1] Perkins' Western Annals, 50.   [2] *Ibid.*
[3] Perkins' Western Annals, 106.   [4] *Ibid.* 108.   [5] *Ibid.* 135.

larger "land States" on the ground that the United States should become a successor to the Crown in title to and jurisdiction over the western lands, the possession of which had been secured through the united forces of the whole Confederacy. Let us briefly treat of this controversy and see how it was settled.

CONSTITUTION OF VIRGINIA AND PROTEST OF MARYLAND.

In June, 1776, Virginia declared in her constitution that "The western and northern extent of Virginia shall in all other respects stand as fixed by the charter of King James the First, in the year one thousand six hundred and nine, and by the public treaty of peace between the courts of Great Britain and France in the year one thousand seven hundred and sixty-three, unless by an act of legislature one or more territories shall hereafter be laid off and governments established west of the Alleghany mountains."[1] This declaration was not well received by the Maryland Convention which met at Annapolis on August 14, 1776, to form a Constitution and Bill of Rights. On October 30, 1776, the Maryland Convention passed the following resolution :

"*Resolved, unanimously,* That it is the opinion of this Convention that the very extensive claim of the State of Virginia to the back lands hath no foundation in justice, and that if the same or any like claim is admitted, the freedom of the smaller States and the liberties of America may be thereby greatly endangered ; this Convention being firmly persuaded that if the dominion over these lands should be established by the blood and treasure of the United States, such lands ought to be considered as a common stock, to be parcelled out at proper times into convenient, free and independent governments."[2] This resolution was afterwards laid before Congress by the delegates of Maryland.

---

[1] Hening's Statutes, Vol. IX, 118.
[2] Conventions of Maryland, 293.

During the whole controversy over the western lands, Virginia was the strongest claimant, while Maryland was the stoutest opponent. The controversy was virtually Maryland *vs.* Virginia, and the contest fairly began in the position assumed by the Maryland Convention in regard to the Constitution of the Old Dominion.

RESOLUTION OF CONGRESS AND MARYLAND'S OPPOSITION.

The Virginia·Constitution was not the only cause that prompted the action of Maryland at the dawn of the Revolution. The resolution of Congress, passed September 16, 1776, must have greatly influenced Maryland in passing her resolution of October 30, 1776.

This resolution of Congress promised both commissioned and non-commissioned officers, who would enlist and serve in the cause of the Revolution, certain bounty lands; to the former, according to rank, from 150 to 500 acres, and to the latter 100 acres, together with a bounty of $20.[1] This policy was by no means agreeable to Maryland. On October 9, 1776, the Maryland Convention resolved "That this State ought not to comply with the proposed terms of granting lands to the officers and soldiers, because there are no lands belonging solely and exclusively to this State; the purchase of lands might eventually involve this State in an expense exceeding its abilities, and an engagement by this State to defray the expense of purchasing land according to its number of souls would be unequal and unjust."[2]

Although Maryland thus differed from Congress in her opinion about the land bounty, and, moreover, complained of the quota of men to be raised according to the whole number of population, including both whites and blacks, yet she was patriotic enough to comply with the wishes of Congress in

---

[1] Journals of Congress, I, 476.
[2] Conventions of Maryland, 272.

regard to the raising of soldiers. But she proposed to give a bounty of ten dollars to every non-commissioned officer and soldier in place of the 100 acres of land promised by Congress. The latter protested against the position Maryland was about to assume in the matter of bounty lands, and assured her that it was the intention of Congress to make good the land bounty at the expense of the United States, and not at the expense of any individual State.

On the 9th of November, 1776, the Maryland Convention passed resolutions in which that body expressed the desire to know the locations of land which Congress would specify as bounty land before any enlistment should be made, and argued again that, from the point of reason, justice, and policy, Congress should consider "the back lands" as a common stock, as being purchased by the joint blood and treasure of the Confederacy. The Convention also expressed its fear that, if the western lands were not made a common property of the nation, and the United States should be obliged to purchase these lands from the larger landed States, these States would fix their own price on the lands, and thus pay off their quota of the public debt, and establish extensive colonies with their own soldiers, much to the detriment of the smaller States.[1] These resolutions were laid before Congress, November 13, 1776.

Thus, the resolution of Congress had greatly influenced Maryland in her attitude toward the "Crown Lands." Out of the eighty-eight battalions of soldiers which Congress aimed to raise, Maryland had its quota of eight battalions. Congress pledged the faith of the United States to soldiers for bounty lands, but it had at that time no lands actually belonging to the Confederacy. Should Congress fail to grant lands, Maryland felt responsible to the pledge, so far as her own men were concerned, but she also had no land of her own. If Congress had been obliged to purchase lands from the

---

[1] Conventions of Maryland, 370–2.

larger landed States, the policy would have resulted in putting a certain portion of Maryland's tax into the treasuries of the landed States, or in reducing their quota of contribution to the common treasury.   On the other hand, if Maryland should become responsible for the promise of Congress, in her individual capacity, to the men who should compose eight battalions, she would find herself at the mercy of the larger States in purchasing lands.   This would not only directly enrich the treasury of the larger States, but also supply soldier-emigrants to the western lands, both of which economic losses Maryland could not afford.   Therefore she proceeded to substitute a bounty of ten dollars for a bounty of 100 acres of land; but Congress remonstrated against this action as "extremely detrimental" to the States, and Maryland had to raise soldiers according to the continental plan of land bounties.   She obeyed the order of Congress, and on December 1, 1776, 2,280 men of Maryland enlisted in the army on the good faith of the United States.[1]

GROUND OF MARYLAND'S OPPOSITION TO VIRGINIA.

The only proper way left for Maryland to protect her own interest, as well as to make good the Federal promise of land bounty, was to persuade Congress to treat the Western lands as common property of the whole nation, to be disposed of by the Federal Government for the benefit of the United States.   It is impossible to say whether or not Maryland, at this early hour of the Revolution, had foreseen, from a purely political standpoint, the necessity of committing the jurisdiction over the Western lands to Congress and of erecting territorial governments under its authority, thus cementing the Union more closely and establishing a fundamental constitution, a "charter of compact," between the original States and Territories.   This national idea, however,

---

[1] Scharf's History of Maryland, 290.

seems not to have been the chief ground of Maryland's opposition to Virginia's land claims. The existing economic situation seems to have led Maryland to assume that position which she so boldly maintained during the whole period of the controversy.

Maryland's opposition to the claim of Virginia was for her indeed a necessity. It was necessary for self-preservation. Her interest required that the Western lands should belong to the United States rather than to Virginia. Should they belong to Virginia, Maryland thought that her freedom would be endangered. She feared that her independence would be placed at the mercy of her powerful neighbor. Maryland's persistent opposition was, therefore, a decidedly prudential and politic measure. Its true nature was defensive, but not offensive. In the defensive measure originated that "pioneer thought"[1] of expanding republican institutions over the Western territory.

On April 18, 1777, the Maryland Legislature instructed their delegates in Congress "to move for a stricter union and confederacy of the thirteen United States."[2] On October 2, 1777, the Articles of Confederation were taken up and debated till November 15, when they were finally adopted. It was during this debate that a Maryland delegate moved "that the United States in Congress assembled shall have the sole and exclusive right and power to ascertain and fix the Western boundary of such States as claim to the Mississippi or South Sea, and lay out the land beyond the boundary so ascertained into separate and independent States, from time to time, as the numbers and circumstances of the people may require."[3] The motion was lost. Not only was it lost, but it resulted in a counter measure; for a provision was added to the Ninth Article of the Confederation that "no State shall be deprived of territory for the benefit of the

---

[1] H. B. Adams. Maryland's Influence upon Land Cessions, 23.
[2] Scharf's History of Maryland, 467.
[3] Journals of Congress, II, 290.

United States."[1]   Thus, by the Constitution, territories were
to be given up to the States that claimed them.   It was a
discouraging case for Maryland.

Within the two succeeding years all the States except
Maryland ratified the Articles, and Maryland knew that she
was at odds, but stood her ground unflinchingly.   When
Maryland laid before Congress her resolutions of October 30,
1776, she was protesting against the aggressive policy of
Virginia alone, but now she found herself in a situation of
fighting the battle against the whole Confederacy.   She was
certainly in a worse situation than before.

On May 21, 1779, the delegates from Maryland laid
before Congress the famous " Instructions " of December 15,
1778.   The document instructed the delegates not to agree
to the Confederation unless they had secured an article or
articles that should guarantee land-cessions.[2]

On the same day the Instructions were issued, the
Legislature of Maryland adopted a " Declaration," which
was sent, together with the Instructions, to the delegates.[3]
On January 6, 1779, the Declaration was laid before Congress.[4]
The Declaration was a compendium of various resolutions
passed by Maryland since the Western lands became a
problem in 1776.   These instruments had great influence
upon Congress in favor of Maryland's cause.   They were a
pivot upon which the question of the land-cession finally
turned toward an amicable solution.

VIRGINIA AND HER DISPOSITION OF WESTERN LANDS.

Meanwhile Virginia passed various land laws, and was
about to establish a Land Office.[5]   This act of the Virginia

[1] Journals of Congress, II, 304.

[2] The text of the Instructions can be found in Journals of Congress, III,
281 ; also in Public Domain, 61-62.

[3] Hening's Statutes, X, 549.

[4] H. B. Adams.   Maryland's Influence on Land Cessions, 27.

[5] Hening's Statutes, X, 50-65.

Legislature must have prompted the action of the Maryland delegates in Congress to lay before that body their Instructions, as well as to introduce the resolution of October 30, 1779. The resolution was passed by a vote of eight States to three, and read as follows :

"*Whereas*, The appropriation of vacant lands by the several States during the continuance of the war will, in the opinion of Congress, be attended with great mischiefs. Therefore

"*Resolved*, That it be earnestly recommended to the State of Virginia to reconsider their late Act of Assembly for opening their Land Office ; and that it be recommended to the said State, and all other States similarly circumstanced, to forbear settling or issuing warrants for unappropriated lands, or granting the same during the continuance of the present war."[1]

But the Virginia Land Court was already opened in Kentucky, and had adjusted about 3,000 claims during its short session. The Virginia Land Laws were very elaborate.[2] They did not recognize the claims of the great land companies, which were then making appeals to Congress for the adjustment of their claims. They encouraged settlement through favorable land grants.

Against the resolution of Congress, which was passed on October 30, 1779, and against the declaration and the instructions of Maryland, Virginia sent her remonstrance.[3] In this remonstrance, Virginia protested against jurisdiction and the right of adjudication which Congress had assumed over the Western lands with regard to the claims of the Vandalia and Indiana Companies. It also affirmed that the royal charter was the only rule to determine the boundaries of each State, and that the United States held no territory save through the right of some one individual State in the Union. It further stated that the Articles of the Con-

---

[1] Journals of Congress, III, 384.
[2] Perkins' Western Annals, 219.
[3] Hening's Statutes, 557–59.

federation reserved to her the right of sovereignty and jurisdiction within her borders, and that she did not entertain any idea of expanding her territory, but of holding her own as defined in the new Constitution.   But the remonstrance took a somewhat compromising attitude, and expressed that Virginia would listen to any just and reasonable propositions for removing the *ostensible* causes of delay to the complete ratification of the Confederation, although she should protest against actions of Congress that were unwarranted by the Articles of Confederation and infringed upon the sovereignty of the State.

Settlement of the Land Controversy.

Notwithstanding the remonstrance of Virginia, Maryland's influence began to be felt among the members of the Union. On February 19, 1780, the New York Legislature passed an act " to facilitate the completion of the Articles of Confederation and perpetual Union among the United States of America," and authorized the delegates from that State to limit her Western boundaries, and cede the vacant lands to the United States.   On March 7, 1780, the above act was laid before Congress by the delegates of New York.[1]

On September 6, 1780, Congress took into consideration the report of the committee to which had been referred the Instructions and Declaration of Maryland, the Remonstrance of Virginia, and the Act of New York, and passed the following resolution: " *Resolved*, That copies of the several papers referred to the committee be transmitted, with a copy of the report, to the legislatures of the several States, and that it be earnestly recommended to those States which have claims to the Western country, to pass such laws and give their delegates in Congress such powers as may effectually remove the only obstacle to a final ratification of the

---

[1] Public Domain, 63.

Articles of Confederation; and that the Legislature of Maryland be earnestly requested to authorize the delegates in Congress to subscribe the said articles."[1]

Mr. Madison wrote to Edmund Pendleton under the date of September 12, 1780, as follows: "Congress have at length entered seriously on a plan for finally ratifying the Confederation. Convinced of the necessity of such a measure, . . . they have recommended, in the most pressing terms, to the States claiming unappropriated back lands, to cede a liberal portion of them for the general benefit. As these exclusive claims formed the only obstacle with Maryland, there is no doubt that a compliance with this recommendation will bring her into the Confederation."[2] Maryland, however, did not at once comply with the resolution, but waited for the compliance of the landed States.

On October 10, 1780, Connecticut tendered a cession of her claims, with certain restrictions as to jurisdiction which were rejected by Congress. On the same day, Congress resolved "that the unappropriated lands that may be ceded or relinquished to the United States by any particular State, pursuant to the recommendation of Congress of the sixth day of September last, shall be disposed of for the common benefit of the United States, and be settled and formed into distinct Republican States, which shall become members of the Federal Union and have the same rights of sovereignty, freedom and independence as the other States; that each State which shall be so formed shall contain a suitable extent of territory, not less than one hundred, nor more than one hundred and fifty miles square, or as near thereto as circumstances will admit. . . . . That the said lands shall be granted or settled at such times and under such regulations as shall hereafter be agreed on by the United States in Congress assembled, or any one or more of them."[3]

---

[1] Journals of Congress, III, 516.
[2] Madison Papers, I, 50.
[3] Journals of Congress, III, 535.

These resolutions were a precursor of the Ordinance of 1784. They defined the ultimate object of disposition which Congress should make of territories to be ceded. On January 2, 1781, the Legislature of Virginia passed an act and offered to cede to the Confederation the long-disputed Western lands on certain conditions which were not satisfactory to Congress.[1] The object of the cession was to complete the ratification of the Articles of the Confederation, and, in case any State yet remained without making the ratification, the cession was to be void.

The three important questions in the early constitutional history of the United States are: 1. The proper mode of voting in Congress, whether by States or according to population or wealth, or *ratio of representation;* 2. The rule by which the expenses of the Union should be appropriated among the States, or *finance;* and 3. The distribution of the vacant and unpatented Western lands, or the *public domain.* That the latter became an important constitutional question was mainly through Maryland's persistent efforts.

But as Congress now urgently requested Maryland to ratify the Articles, and New York and Virginia, as well as Connecticut, offered to cede the Western lands, and, furthermore, Maryland's attitude gave some hope to Great Britain that the Confederation might fail through domestic dissensions of the States, Maryland could no longer withhold the ratification, although no one of the proposed cessions was acceptable to her. Consequently, on January 29, 1781, the Maryland Legislature passed an act to empower her delegates in Congress to subscribe and ratify the Articles of the Confederation, which was read in Congress on February 12, 1781, and on March 1, 1781, the delegates of Maryland signed the Articles.

Maryland's ratification seems to have occasioned great rejoicing throughout the States. Mr. Duane wrote to Wash-

---

[1] Public Domain, 67.

ington to this effect: "Let us devote this day to joy and congratulation, since by the accomplishment of a Federal Union we are become a nation. In a political view, it is of more real importance than a victory over all our enemies."[1] The very day Maryland joined the Confederation the delegates of New York made in Congress a formal offer of her Western lands. It took, however, another year for Congress to determine to accept any of the offers of Western lands, for politics and party feelings, especially with regard to the admission of Vermont, largely entered into the long-vexed question.

On May 1, 1782, a committee to whom the cessions of New York, Virginia, and Connecticut and the petitions of the several land companies had been referred, made a report favorable to the acceptance of the cession offered by New York. Among the reasons assigned by the committee, it was said "that, by Congress accepting this cession, the jurisdiction of the whole Western territory belonging to the Six Nations and their tributaries will be vested in the United States, greatly to the advantage of the Union."[2] The committee also reported that Congress should recommend Massachusetts and Connecticut to cede their claims without any conditions or restrictions whatsoever. Regarding the cession proposed by Virginia, the committee reported that the conditions annexed to the cession were incompatible with the honor, interests, and peace of the United States, and that Congress should neither accept the cession nor guarantee the tract of country claimed by Virginia.

On October 29, 1782, the delegates of Maryland moved that Congress should accept all the right, title, interest, jurisdiction, and claim of New York as ceded by the agents of that State on March 1, 1781. Virginia and Massachusetts voted in the negative, and the Carolinas were divided,

---

[1] Bancroft. Constitutional History of United States, I, 17.
[2] Journals of Congress, IV, 22.

while Georgia was not represented. All the rest of the Union voted in the affirmative. So the cession of New York was finally accepted by Congress. This was just six years after Maryland issued her first protest against Virginia's land claims. The land question did not then promise to become an important national problem, but now the whole Union beheld the creation of a public domain out of the ceded lands in which common economic interests were permanently to abide.

On September 13, 1783, a committee to whom the cession of Virginia and the report thereon were referred reported that Virginia's claim to the guaranty of its southeastern boundary and to the annulling of the claims of all other titles to the northwestern territory was unreasonable, and that Virginia should waive all these obnoxious conditions, when the cession would be acceptable by Congress.[1] Virginia modified the conditions of her cession, but still claimed all her chartered rights. On October 20, 1783, Virginia empowered her delegates in Congress to make the cession, which was consummated by the deed of transfer signed by Jefferson, Monroe, and others on March 1, 1784.[2]

Massachusetts and Connecticut soon followed Virginia. The Massachusetts cession took place on April 19, 1785, and that of Connecticut on September 14, 1786. Connecticut, in her deed of cession, reserved a tract of lands lying in the northeastern portion of the State of Ohio known as the "Western Reserve of Connecticut in Ohio," which, together with the "Fire Lands" now lying in the counties of Erie, Huron, and Ottawa, in Ohio, contained about 3,800,000 acres. On May 30, 1800, Connecticut ceded to Congress the entire jurisdiction over her "Western Reserve."

---

[1] Journals of Congress, IV, 263.
[2] *Ibid.* 342.

CESSIONS OF THE SOUTHEASTERN TERRITORY.

We have thus far noticed the cessions of the territory northwest of the Ohio River, as they are important not only in the history of the Public Domain, but also in the history of American constitutional development. The subject of land-cessions by the States, however, will not have been completely treated without some notice of the cession of territory southeast of the Ohio. But there is nothing particularly interesting in the cessions made by the three Southern States. The facts can be stated in a few words.

/ On March 8, 1787, South Carolina offered to Congress to cede her Western claim, and Congress accepted the cession on August 9, 1787. The territory ceded by South Carolina is a narrow strip of land which extends from the northwestern boundary of South Carolina to the Mississippi, and which now forms the extreme northern portion of the States of Georgia, Alabama, and Mississippi. It contains an area of 4,900 square miles.[1]

/ The next Southern State that ceded her territory was North Carolina. Her cession was accepted by Congress on April 2, 1790. The cession constituted the present State of Tennessee. In accepting the cession offered by North Carolina, Congress made a poor bargain. In the deed of cession North Carolina stated certain conditions by which Congress had to satisfy a number of claims before it should make any disposition of the ceded lands. It proved afterward that Congress could hardly make any disposition whatever of the acquired land, for the claims were even in excess of lands whose Indian title had been extinguished by that State. Being thus covered by reservations, the cession made by North Carolina was only nominal, and no public lands were created out of the ceded territory.

The last State that made cession of her Western lands was Georgia. This State made her first movement toward cession

---

[1] Public Domain, 76.

on February 5, 1788, but her cession was not accepted by Congress. Here, for the first time in the history of the Land Cession, we meet with conflicting claims on the part of the National and of the State Government. The cession as proposed by Georgia in 1788 included the territory lying between 31° and 32° 30′ north latitude. The eastern boundary-line began with the western extremity of Georgia, and the western limit was the Mississippi River, as in the case of other State claims. This territory was in the province of British West Florida, which was ceded by Great Britain to the United States in 1783. Consequently, the United States claimed the right of jurisdiction over this territory.

In the meantime the Legislature of Georgia sold 13,500,-000 acres of lands in the Mississippi Territory to certain Yazoo Companies. The lands thus sold were not within the limits of the State of Georgia, but in the territory whose title belonged to the United States according to the treaty of 1783. The Yazoo Companies sold out their claims to the lands, and various new companies were organized under such sales. In February, 1796, the Legislature of Georgia passed an act and annulled the sale of the Yazoo Companies to several land companies for the lands west of the river Chattahoochee. Thus arose the litigation for lands in Georgia.

On April 7, 1798, Congress passed an act authorizing the President to appoint three commissioners to settle the conflicting claims of the United States, and to receive the cession of Georgia. The United States Commissioners and the Commissioners of Georgia came finally to an agreement, and on April 24, 1802, Georgia ceded her entire Western claims. The ceded territory was estimated at 88,578 square miles. The Georgian cession cost the United States in all about $6,200,000, as it was encumbered with various land claims.

The following table shows the dates and area of cessions by the States:

TABLE I.

States.	Date.	Square Miles.	Acres.
Massachusetts, } Cessions Connecticut, } disputed....	April 19, 1785 Sept. 13, 1786	54,000 40,000	34,560,000 25,600,000
New York—Actual............	March 1, 1781	315.91	202,187
Virginia—Exclusive of K...	March 1, 1784	265,562.00	169,959,680
South Carolina........... ...	August 9, 1787	4.900.00	3,136,000
North Carolina...........	Feb. 25, 1790	45,000.00	29,184,000
Georgia.........	April 24, 1802	88,578.00	56,689,920
Total Cession............		404,955.91	259,171,787

Table II. shows where the ceded lands are now located :

TABLE II.

Ceding States.		States.	Areas.
New York......		Erie, Penn.	351.91
Virginia.........		Ohio.	39,964.00
Virginia, Massachusetts and Connecticut........	} Northwest of the River Ohio.........	Indiana.	33,809.00
		Illinois.	35,414.00
		Michigan.	56,451.00
		Wisconsin.	53,924.00
	265,877.91 sq. m.	Minnesota.	26,000.00
South Carolina............	}	Georgia.	1,500.00
		Alabama.	1,700.00
	{ Southeast of the	Mississippi.	1,700.00
	River Ohio.........	Tennessee.	45,600.00
North Carolina......	} 139,078 sq. m.	Alabama.	46,722.00
Georgia.........	J	Mississippi.	41,856.00
Total Area............			404,955.91

We have now come to the second great acquisition of territory by the United States—viz. :

THE PURCHASE OF LOUISIANA.

We have seen that the public lands were created by cessions from the States, but we must keep in mind that the creation of the public lands was not accompanied by an increase of area in national domain, for the cessions were within the national domain and of definite extent and character. The transaction was within one household, and the transfer of ownership was from members of the same household to a representative head of all. The purchase of Louisiana was an international transaction. It was a dealing with foreign soil belonging to a foreign sovereign. It was an acquisition that was accompanied by a vast increase of area in national as well as in public domain. The whole acquisition became public lands, out of which eleven commonwealths and six territories have already sprung.[1] The new territory was no less than eleven hundred and eighty thousand square miles, being five times greater than the area of France.

Indeed, the purchase of Louisiana was the most important acquisition the United States has ever made. The possession of a vast empire west of the Mississippi, and the advantages of free, untrammeled river navigation, have made the United States a truly great power in the world. Supposing France or Spain had control of the great central valleys of the Mississippi and Missouri Rivers. In the southeast lies New Orleans, a key to the great water-course to which the United States could not have had access. Far up along the Pacific Coast lie now the Territory of Washington and the State of Oregon, whose land once belonged to the province of Louisiana. A little lower down the coast there is the State of California, with its rich gold-mines and its capacious harbor. Supposing a great Latin empire had arisen in this province of Louisiana. California, with its gold-mines; Nevada and Colorado, with their silver; New Mexico and Texas with their agricultural resources, would not now belong to the United States. The great West, with all its natural wealth and resources, would now be subject to European powers. The territory back of the Alleghanies and east of the Mississippi, which was the first curtailment of French claims, might, in the chances of war and politics, have undergone a retroces-

---

[1] Public Domain, 105.

sion to France or a total loss to Spain, and the United States
have remained pent up, confined along Atlantic borders. The
United States, of such a character, would have been entirely
different from the United States of to-day. Good policy, prudential measures, and the final purchase of Louisiana, made the
United States the master of the best portions of the New
World. Let us now briefly review the history of the purchase
of Louisiana by the United States.

History of Settlement in Louisiana.

The name Louisiana was originally applied to a vast
region of an unknown extent back of the Alleghany Mountains, and along the Mississippi River and its tributaries.
Of indefinite and ambiguous character, French Louisiana
was much like the English Virginia, and, like the latter, it
had to undergo several curtailments, until it assumed a definite
historical character.

In 1683, La Salle christened the country in honor of Louis
XIV. The French cavalier performed a baptismal duty
similar to that discharged by the English courtier, Sir
Walter Raleigh, when he christened Virginia in honor of the
virgin queen Elizabeth. Both adventurers failed, however,
in their colonial enterprise. La Salle met with scarcely a
better fate than the luckless Raleigh, for he was shot by
one of his own men on a relief expedition to Canada. The
task of first organizing Louisiana for economic purposes fell
upon Sieur Antoine Crozat; and Louis XIV. granted a
charter for commercial privileges in Louisiana.[1] The charter
was surrendered by Crozat in 1717, and in the same year
it was granted to the "Company of the West."[2]

The French domination in Louisiana lasted till November
3, 1762, when it was ceded to Spain. On February 10, 1763,
France and Spain ceded all their possessions in North

---

[1] Historical Collections of Louisiana, III, 38.
[2] *Ibid.* 49.

America east of the Mississippi River, except New Orleans[1] and the island on which it stands. The Mississippi River was fixed as an international boundary between the Spanish Louisiana and the English colonies. On October 1, 1800, Spain, by the secret treaty of San Ildefonso, transferred the Province of Louisiana back to France. Spain ceded Louisiana to France in consideration of the Grand Duchy of Tuscany, then granted to the Duke of Parma, the son-in-law of the King of Spain, and dreamed little of the sale of Louisiana by Bonaparte to the United States. The Spanish domination in Louisiana lasted for thirty-eight years. But a third power was to replace both France and Spain in that interesting historical Province of Louisiana.

PECULIARITIES IN THE INSTITUTIONS OF LOUISIANA.

Before proceeding farther in the history of the acquisition of Louisiana by the United States, let us notice some of the peculiarities which that province presented to the world in point of institutions, laws, and population. At the outbreak of the French and Indian war, France possessed the territorial basis of a splendid empire in the new world. Her possessions embraced, on the south, the mouth of the Mississippi, on the north, that of the St. Lawrence. Her territory stretched through the heart of the continent and covered the great central valley of the Mississippi and the Northern Lakes. The peace of Paris in 1763, as we have seen, curtailed this grand possession. A vast Western empire was divided by the Mississippi into English and Spanish dominions.

Although Louisiana was thus successively an imperial province of the French and Spanish monarchies, it is said that feudalism never prevailed there. "Louisiana never knew anything like a right of primogeniture and a privileged

---

[1] New Orleans was named in honor of Philip, Duke of Orleans, Regent from 1715 to 1723, during the minority of Louis XV.

class. No part of feudality was ever known here, neither in equality in the distribution of estates nor fiefs nor seignories nor mayoralties. The grants of land were all allodial, and under no other condition than that of cultivation and improvement within limited periods; in fact, essentially in fee-simple."[1]

Though Louisiana did not inherit feudalism, it inherited French law and custom. They were introduced through the charter granted to Crozat. The charter says that "our edicts, ordinances and customs, and the usages of the mayor-alty and shrievalty of Paris shall be observed for laws and customs in the said country of Louisiana."[2] The matri-monial community of gains, the inalienability of dower, the strict guards by which the property-rights of the wife were secured against the extravagance of spendthrift husbands, were all introduced into Louisiana, and reveal the French inheritance of Roman law. The writ of *habeas corpus* and trial by jury were unknown in the Louisiana of French and Spanish domination. The introduction of the Spanish law in 1769 did not materially change the French laws and customs.

During the thirty-eight years of Spanish rule, Louisiana greatly increased in population. It was "the favored part of Spain." In sixteen years from 1769 the population of Louisiana is said to have doubled,[3] but the population represented different nationalities. "Like the rich soil upon our great rivers," says Dr. Billard, "the population may be said to be alluvial, composed of distinctly colored strata, not yet perfectly amalgamated, left by successive waves of emigration. Here we trace the gay, light-hearted, brave chivalry of France; the more impassionate and devoted Spaniard; the untiring industry and perseverance of the German, and the bluff sturdiness of the British race. Here

[1] Historical Collections of Louisiana, I, 15.
[2] Public Domain, 90.
[3] Historical Collections of Louisiana, 15.

were thrown the wreck of Acadie, and the descendants of these unhappy fugitives still exist in various parts of the country. . . . . The traces of the Canadian hunter and boatman are not yet entirely erased."[1]

AMERICAN DIPLOMACY IN THE PURCHASE OF LOUISIANA.

In a territory where there were such laws and customs, and such a cosmopolitan population, Napoleon aimed to establish the new *régime* of France in the nineteenth century. This was "viewed with great alarm in the United States." No sooner was Mr. Jefferson inaugurated than he began to look into the matter of the secret cession of Spain. On March 29, 1801, Mr. King, then the American Minister in London, informed the Government of the cession of Louisiana.[2] Thereby, Mr. Pinckney, at Madrid, and Mr. Livingstone, at Paris, were instructed with regard to the alleged transfer. On November 20, 1801, Mr. King sent from London a copy of a treaty signed at Madrid, by which the Prince of Parma was established in Tuscany. This was the confirmation of the secret treaty of San Ildefonso, and the secrecy of the transfer of Louisiana became an open and acknowledged fact.

Regarding seriously this transfer of Louisiana to France, Mr. Jefferson, under the date of April 18, 1802, wrote to Mr. Livingstone as follows: " The cession of Louisiana and the Floridas by Spain to France works most sorely on the United States. . . . It completely reverses all the political relations of the United States, and will form a new epoch in our political course. . . . There is on the globe one single spot the possessor of which is our natural and habitual enemy. It is New Orleans, through which the produce of three-eighths of our territory must pass to market, and from

---

[1] Historical Collections of Louisiana, I, 4.
[2] American State Papers, II, 509.

its fertility it will ere long yield more than half of our whole produce, and contain more than half of our inhabitants. France, placing herself in that door, assumes to us the attitude of defiance. The day that France takes possession of New Orleans fixes the sentence which is to restrain her for ever within her low-water mark. From that moment we must marry ourselves to the British fleet and nation." Mr. Jefferson further instructed Livingstone to persuade the French Government to part with New Orleans in order that peace and friendship might continue between the two nations.[1] Accordingly, Mr. Livingstone made efforts to convince the French Government that its true interest demanded the selling of French possessions in America,[2] but, at first, Bonaparte would not listen to this idea.

On October 16, 1802, Don Morales, Spanish intendant of Louisiana, prohibited the further use by the United States of the city of New Orleans as a place of deposit for merchandise, as guaranteed by the treaty of 1795. The twenty-second article of the same treaty stipulated that, in case Spain should withdraw the right of use by the United States of New Orleans, she was to assign another place, on another part of the banks of the Mississippi, in lieu of New Orleans. The Spanish intendant failed to do so, and, throughout the United States, great excitement followed his act.

It seems to have been the policy of Spain that foreign commerce should be excluded from the Mississippi River. In the treaty of 1783, it was agreed between Great Britain and the United States that the navigation of the Mississippi should be free to both nations.[3] But Spain was in possession of the territory west of the river, as well as of New Orleans and the island on which it stands. The southern boundary of the United States was fixed at the thirty-first parallel of north latitude. Spain refused to make a treaty with the

---

[1] Jefferson's Works, IV, 432–34.

[2] American State Papers, II, 520–25.

[3] Laws of U. S. (Duane edition), I, 205.

United States in 1780–82, for Jay demanded the free navigation of the Mississippi.

On October 27, 1795, Pinckney succeeded in concluding
a treaty by which the southern boundary of the United
States was recognized as 31° north latitude, and the free
navigation of the Mississippi and the right of deposit in
New Orleans were assured to the United States by Spain.
With regard to the place of deposit, however, the United
States was at Spain's mercy.   New Orleans was guaranteed
for three years only, and whether or not the port might be
used afterward depended upon the pleasure of the King of
Spain.   The Spanish intendant closed New Orleans to the
citizens of the United States, and their interests were thus
imperilled.   If 'France should come into possession of New
Orleans, the interests of the United States would be even
more endangered.

Mr. Jefferson therefore determined to get hold of New
Orleans and the Floridas by peaceful negotiations, in spite
of the opposition of the war-party in Congress.   On January
10, 1803, Mr. Monroe was appointed as Minister Pleni-
potentiary and Envoy Extraordinary to France, and $2,000,-
000 were appropriated for the purposes of his mission.
Joining with the American Ministers at Paris and Madrid,
Mr. Monroe had to open negotiations anew for the acquisition
of New Orleans and the Floridas.

The acquisition of the province of Louisiana west of the
Mississippi was not yet thought of by Mr. Jefferson and his
Cabinet.   Under the date of January 13, 1803, Mr. Jefferson
wrote to Mr. Monroe on his nomination and the policy of the
Government regarding the subject of purchasing New Orleans
as follows: "The agitation of the public mind on occasion of
the late suspension of our right of deposit at New Orleans is
extreme.   In the Western country it is natural, and grounded
on honest motives.   In the seaports it proceeds from a desire
for war, which increases the mercantile lottery; in the
Federalists generally, and especially those of Congress, the

object is to force us into war, if possible, in order to derange our finances, or, if this cannot be done, to attach the Western country to them as their best friends, and thus get again into power. Remonstrances, memorials, etc., are now circulating through the whole of the Western country, and signed by the body of the people. The measures we have been pursuing, being invisible, do not satisfy their minds. Something sensible, therefore, has become necessary; and indeed our object of purchasing New Orleans and the Floridas is a measure liable to assume so many shapes that no instructions could be squared to fit them. It was essential, then, to send a Minister Extraordinary, to be joined with the ordinary one, with discretionary powers. . . . . All eyes, all hopes, are now fixed on you; and were you to decline, the chagrin would be universal, and would shake under your feet the high ground on which you stand with the public. Indeed, I know nothing which would produce such a shock. For on the event of this mission depend the future destinies of this republic."[1] The entire correspondence of **Mr. Jefferson** shows that he regarded the acquisition of Louisiana as necessary to the United States in order to preserve peace at home and friendship abroad. His pacific policy finally proved of great benefit to the Union.

Just before the arrival of **Mr. Monroe, M. Talleyrand** requested Mr. Livingstone to make an offer for the whole Province of Louisiana. Mr. Livingstone intimated that 20,000,000 francs would be a fair price, but that sum was considered too little by the French Minister. It was not the intention of the United States to purchase entire Louisiana, and Mr. Livingstone had really no authority to negotiate for it. The instructions to Mr. Livingstone and Mr. Monroe on March 2, 1803, gave a plan which expressly left to France "all her territory on the west side of the Mississippi."[2] France, however, wanted to dispose of the whole Province of

[1] Jefferson's Works, IV, 454.
[2] American State Papers, II, 540–44.

Louisiana. On April 12, 1803, Mr. Monroe arrived in Paris. The next day M. Barbé Marbois, the Minister of the Treasury, opened the negotiation with the two American Ministers, who offered him, on behalf of the United States, 50,000,000 francs. This sum was refused, for Napoleon wanted 125,000,000 francs. In this negotiation the American Ministers were acting beyond their instructions.

There were rumors of England's intention to capture Louisiana. Quick negotiation was therefore needed. Napoleon had previously intended to send the French fleet at San Domingo to Louisiana, in order to take possession of it. Should the negotiation fail, he might renew his object. Besides, the treaty of San Ildefonso had a restrictive clause touching the alienation of Louisiana, and should Spain learn of the intention of Bonaparte she might interfere with the negotiation, and the plan of Mr. Jefferson might consequently fail.

Fear of English capture and of Spanish interference, on the one hand, and, on the other, the proposition of the French Government, which was beyond ministerial instructions, were pressing considerations with Messrs. Livingstone and Monroe. Their political good sense must decide what course to pursue for the benefit of the United States. They finally accepted the proposition of M. Marbois to take the whole Province of Louisiana for 80,000,000 francs, one-fourth of which sum was assigned to the payment of the claims of American citizens against the French Government, in case they should amount to that figure. The cession was made April 30, 1803, with three separate provisions: First, a treaty of cession; second, a convention as to the payment of purchase-money; and third, a convention as to the settlement of the American claims against the French Government.[1] On October 19, 1803, the Senate ratified the treaty, and ratifications were exchanged at Washington two days later. On October 23, 1803, the President was authorized

---

[1] See Public Domain, 96-99, for these treaties.

to take possession of the ceded territory, which was not yet in the hands of the French. On November 30, 1803, however, Pierre Clement Laussat, the French Commissioner, received the Province of Louisiana from El Marquez de Casa Calvo, the Spanish Commissioner, and after an occupation of twenty days, France, on December 20, 1803, ceded Louisiana to the United States.

UNCONSTITUTIONALITY OF THE LOUISIANA PURCHASE.

Mr. Jefferson freely admitted that his act was unauthorized by the Constitution. In a letter to Breckenridge under the date of August 12, 1803, he says: "This treaty [referring to the treaty of cession] must, of course, be laid before both Houses, because both have important functions to exercise respecting it. They, I presume, will see their duty to their country in ratifying and paying for it, so as to secure a good which would otherwise probably be never again in their power. But I suppose they must then appeal to *the nation* for an additional article to the Constitution, approving and confirming an act which the nation had not previously authorized. The Constitution has made no provision for our holding foreign territory, still less for incorporating foreign nations into our Union. The Executive, in seizing the fugitive occurrences which so much advance the good of their country, had done an act beyond the Constitution: The Legislature, in casting behind them metaphysical subtleties, and risking themselves like faithful servants, must ratify and pay for it, and throw themselves on their country for doing for them unauthorized what we know they would have done for themselves had they been in a situation to do it." [1] Indeed, the entire party connected with the purchase had done a thing unauthorized. The Ministers abroad went far beyond their instructions. The President, knowing the

---

[1] Jefferson's Works, IV, 500-501.

unconstitutionality of the purchase, deliberately made it for the good of the country and with faith in the nation. Congress took the part of a "guardian" and invested the people's money in Louisiana, but with no constitutional authority. The result justified the act, and the nation acquiesced and rejoiced in the acquisition of the new territory.

SPANISH PROTEST AGAINST THE CESSION OF LOUISIANA.

It was Spain that fared worst in the transaction between France and the United States. The day on which Spain secretly transferred Louisiana back to France determined the destiny of the Spanish colonies in North America. She was bound to lose them, either by cession or by revolution. Spain protested against the cession of Louisiana to the United States, but the protest availed nothing. Mr. Jefferson wrote to Mr. Livingstone, under the date of November 4, 1803, that "Spain had entered with us a protestation against our ratification of the treaty, grounded, first, on the assertion that the First Consul had not executed the conditions of the treaties of cession; and, secondly, that he had broken a solemn promise not to alienate the country to any nation. We answered that these were private questions between France and Spain which they must settle together; that we derived our title from the First Consul, and did not doubt his guarantee of it."[1] There appear to have been some rumors that Spain would not deliver the whole Province of Louisiana to France, and Mr. Pinckney, the American Minister at Madrid, made inquiry of the Spanish Government, which assured him that the King had given no order whatever for opposing the delivery of Louisiana to the French, and that he had thought proper to renounce his protest against the alienation of Louisiana by France, notwithstanding the solid grounds upon which that protest was founded; affording in this way a new proof of his benevolence and friendship for the United States.[2]

---

[1] Jefferson's Works, IV, 511.   [2] Public Domain, 104.

Spain thus renounced her claim to Louisiana, but the boundary-lines between Louisiana and the Spanish Floridas were not fixed till 1819. Spain claimed that the portion of territory lying below 31° north latitude, and between the Iberville and Perdido Rivers, was within the limits of West Florida. The United States claimed that this territory was within the ancient boundary of Louisiana, and was therefore a part of the cession by Spain to France by the treaty of San Ildefonso, which part, by virtue of the treaty of 1803, should now come under the jurisdiction of the United States. This controversy, known as "Perdido Claim," was settled by the cession of Florida to the United States by Spain in 1819, although the former disregarded the Spanish claim, and actually took possession of the territory before that date.

The following table shows the cost and area of the Louisiana Purchase, as well as its subsequent division into the States and Territories.

TABLE III.[1]

THE LOUISIANA PURCHASE.

Principal..	$15,000,000.00
Interest to redemption...	8,529,353.00
	$23,529,353.00
The French Spoliation Claims paid by the United States...	3,738,268.98
Total cost of Louisiana Purchase........................	$27,267,621.98

	Area in Square Miles.
Alabama: between the Perdido and State of Mississippi...............	2,300
Mississippi: between Alabama and Louisiana, below 31° N......	3,600
Louisiana..	41,346
Arkansas..	52,202
Missouri...	65,370
Kansas: all but southwest corner..............................	73,542
Iowa..	55,045
Amount carried forward	293,405

[1] Public Domain, 105.

Amount brought forward.......................................	293,405
Minnesota : west of the Mississippi River....................	57,531
Nebraska..	75,995
Colorado: east of the Rocky Mountains and north of the Arkansas River...	57,000
Oregon...	95,274
Dakota...	150,932
Montana..	143,776
Idaho..	86,294
Washington...	69,994
Wyoming: all but the zone in the middle, south and southwest part...	83,563
Indian Territory...	68,991
Total area of Louisiana Purchase.............................	1,182,755

PURCHASE OF THE FLORIDAS.

As we have already seen, when Mr. Jefferson opened the negotiation through his Ministers with Bonaparte for the purchase of Louisiana, it was not the Province of Louisiana, but rather New Orleans and the Floridas, that he intended to purchase. The fact that Spain did not cede the Floridas was only later known to the United States. Therefore, the offer by Bonaparte of the entire Province of Louisiana was beyond the expectation of Mr. Jefferson.

The correspondence of Mr. Jefferson clearly shows that his original idea was to secure New Orleans and the Floridas, and thus to have for the United States a well-rounded national domain east of the Mississippi. Therefore, Mr. Jefferson must have begun the negotiation with the idea that the territory of West Florida extended as far west as the Mississippi, with 31° north latitude for its northern boundary, as settled in the treaty with Spain of 1795. If it were understood, on the contrary, that West Florida extended only to the Perdido River, then Mr. Jefferson should have given instructions to his Ministers to negotiate the purchase of both Floridas, of New Orleans, and that part of Louisiana east of the Mississippi and lying between the rivers Perdido and Mississippi. But, instead of this, as the instructions were for the purchase of New Orleans and the Floridas, Mr. Jefferson must have taken it for granted that West Florida extended to the Mississippi, as Spain afterward claimed.

GROUNDS OF AMERICAN AND SPANISH DISPUTES.

From the above facts, there seem to be good reasons for the claim of Spain to the tract of territory west of the Perdido River. In the first place, France ceded to Great Britain, in 1763, the territory east of the Mississippi, as well as Canada, and confirmed to Spain the cession of the previous year—namely, the Province of Louisiana west of the Mississippi, with New Orleans and its island. By the same treaty Spain ceded to Great Britain the Province of Florida. Out of these cessions by France and Spain, Great Britain organized, among others, the two provinces of East and West Florida in the southern portion of her newly-acquired territory.

By the treaty of 1783 the southern boundary of the United States was recognized by England as 31° north latitude. But Spain, taking advantage of the American Revolution, wrested from England the provinces of the Floridas. She claimed the British Province of West Florida, whose northern boundary-line ran from the confluence of the Yazoo with the Mississippi on the west to the Appalachicola River on the east, as fixed by the Royal Order to Governor Elliot of May 15, 1767.[1] But, as we have already seen, Spain waived this claim by the treaty of 1795, and recognized the southern boundary of the United States as set forth in the definitive treaty of 1783. This treaty of 1795 settled the boundary dispute of the two nations, and Spain was once more the ruler of the Floridas and the vast empire of Louisiana.

But the secret cession to France by Spain of Louisiana in

---

[1] Laws of the United States (Duane edition), I, 451.

1800, and its purchase from France by the United States in 1803, again brought forth a fresh dispute between the United States and Spain as to the boundary-line between Louisiana and West Florida. Spain claimed the boundary-line as ceded by Great Britain in 1783, to which country France ceded her possessions east of the Mississippi in 1763. The United States claimed the ancient boundary of Louisiana as France had possessed it previous to 1763. Spain argued that France did not cede to her the territory east of the Mississippi in 1763, and that she did not cede back to France in 1800 what France did not cede to her in 1763. All the disputes arose from obscurity in the treaty of 1803 between the United States and France regarding the boundaries of Louisiana. Not only as to the eastern, but also as to the western boundary-line, the United States had a dispute with Spain, to which we shall later refer.

SITUATION OF SPANISH COLONIES AFTER THE LOUISIANA PURCHASE.

By the purchase of Louisiana by the United States, the Spanish colony in Mexico was separated from that in Florida by a growing nation whose interests in the development and settlement of the western country were stronger and more rational than those of an ambitious and capricious nation like the French. Spain was destined to lose both of the colonies. Mr. Jefferson saw that the United States would ultimately succeed in the acquisition of the Floridas, and was fully convinced of the vast importance of the Mississippi navigation. In a private letter to Breckenridge under the date of August 12, 1803, he wrote as follows: " Objections are raising to the eastward against the vast extent of our boundaries, and propositions are made to exchange Louisiana or a part of it for the Floridas. But, as I have said, we shall get the Floridas without, and I would not give one inch of the waters of the Mississippi to any nation, because I see in a light very important to our peace the exclusive right to its navigation and the admission of no nation into it."[1] .... With regard to the boundaries of Louisiana, Mr. Jefferson wrote in the same letter the following : " We have some claims to extend on the seacoast westwardly to the Rio Norte or Bravo, and, better, to go eastwardly to the Rio Perdido, between Mobile and Pensacola, the ancient boundary of Louisiana."

The Perdido claim, however, was not pushed by the United States, but efforts were made to purchase the Floridas from Spain by Armstrong and Bowdoin, Monroe and Pinckney, under instructions from President Jefferson. All negotiations failed. In 1810 a revolutionary party in West Florida declared independence of Spanish rule and formed a State. The independents elected one Rhea for President, and asked of the United States admission to the Union. They further asked for a loan of money, and that the United States would recognize vacant lands in West Florida as the common property of the new commonwealth.[2] President Madison did not grant the requests of the revolutionary party, but issued a proclamation to take possession of the territory east of the Mississippi under the treaty of 1803. Governor Claiborne, of Orleans Territory, was sent there to take possession.

The revolutionists from Fort Stoddart attacked Mobile, which was then held by the Spanish authority, but were repulsed. Another attack was, however, threatened, and, alarmed at the condition of affairs, Tolch, the Spanish Governor, wrote a letter to the American authorities, and intimated that he would transfer the territory to the United States unless he were soon reinforced from Havana or Vera Cruz.

On April 14, 1812, the territory lying between the Pearl and Mississippi Rivers was annexed to Louisiana, and the

---

[1] Jefferson's Works, IV, 499.

[2] Hildreth. History of United States, VI, 223.

remaining portion, as far east as the Perdido River, was incorporated, May 14, 1812, with the Mississippi Territory.

In the meantime a fresh trouble arose in East Florida. By a secret act of Congress, General Mathews, of Georgia, was commissioned to East Florida to receive the province, if the Spanish authority would transfer it by an amicable settlement, or to take possession of the province by force if any foreign power should attempt to seize it. Mathews co-operated with the insurgents and defied the Spanish authorities.[1] Congress disapproved his act, and replaced him by appointing Governor Mitchell, of Georgia. Mitchell pursued the same policy as General Mathews, and did not withdraw the American troops from Florida. The Legislature of Georgia passed an act November 20, 1812, that a State force should be raised to reduce St. Augustine and punish the Indians.[2] They resolved that the occupation of East Florida was essential to the safety of the State, whether Congress should approve their act or not.

Thus Georgia apparently came in conflict with the National Government, but its legislative measure must have coincided with the policy of the administration, which was compelled by the existing state of affairs to resort to military operations, both against the hostile Indians and the British forces now in Spanish territory. On July 14, 1814, General Jackson was ordered to take possession of Pensacola, but before the order reached him a British naval force reached Pensacola and lent aid to the hostile Creeks. Jackson succeeded in driving out the British, and delivered over the town to the Spanish authorities.

In 1816 Don Orris, the Spanish Ambassador, who was recognized as such the previous year, protested against the occupation of West Florida by the United States, and insisted upon non-intercourse between the United States and Mexico,

---

[1] Hildreth. History of the United States, VI, 311.
[2] *Ibid.* 375.

for the latter was now in revolt against Spain.[1]   Mr. Monroe,
then Secretary of State, suggested the transfer of the Floridas
to the United States in exchange for a part of Louisiana
lying near Texas, but nothing resulted from this communi-
cation.

In the following year Mr. Monroe became President, and
proposed the cession of the Floridas by Spain in lieu of the
claims of American citizens against that country, and a
diplomatic correspondence upon this question ensued between
John Quincy Adams and Don Orris.   During the same year
the Seminole Indians harbored Creek refugees and were a
source of trouble to the Georgia settlers.   General Jackson
was ordered to conduct a campaign against the Seminoles,
and was instructed to pursue them into Florida, if necessary.
In April, 1818, Jackson took possession of the Spanish fort
at St. Mark's in Florida, and in the following month he
entered the town of Pensacola.   The Spanish Governor held
the fort at the Barrancas, which capitulated three days later.
On June 17, 1818, Don Orris protested against the action of
General Jackson, but Adams replied that it was justifiable
on the principle of self-defence, and because of the non-fulfilment of the treaty obligation of Spain to restrain the
Indians within her territory.

FORMAL NEGOTIATIONS FOR FLORIDA.

Jackson's military operations in Florida caused hot discussions in Congress, but, while the matter was pending, the
ratification of the convention of 1802 between the United
States and Spain arrived at Washington.   This was a convention for adjusting the mutual claims of each government.
According to instructions received from the Spanish Government in connection with the ratification, Don Orris opened
negotiations for the cession of the Floridas.   There was
some disagreement at first with regard to the western

---

[1] Public Domain, 110.

boundary of Louisiana, but at last a compromise was effected, and on February 22, 1819, a treaty of cession was signed by Adams and Orris.

Mr. Benton, regretting that the western boundary of Louisiana was not extended as far westward into Texas as it ought to be, and remarking the political considerations that entered into the question, said that "the repugnance in the Northeast was not merely to territorial aggrandizement in the Southwest, but to consequent extension of slavery in that quarter; and to allay that repugnance and to prevent the slavery-extension question from becoming a test in the Presidential election was the true reason, for giving away Texas, and the true solution of the enigma involved in the strange refusal to accept as much as Spain offered."[1]

The acquisition of the Floridas and the settlement of the Louisiana boundary seem, however, to have met with popular approval, for Mr. Benton himself declared that he stood "solitary and alone" in this question, and was mortified at finding that not a paper in the United States supported his opposition.

The Orris-Adams Treaty was unanimously ratified by the United States Senate, but Spain hesitated to ratify it, and suffered the time for ratification to elapse. After much correspondence, Spain finally agreed to the treaty, October 29, 1820, and in the following year she surrendered the disputed territory to the United States.

The third and fourth articles in the treaty that related to the western boundary of Louisiana remained a dead letter for many years, because of the war between Mexico and Spain. But when Mexico became independent, the United States entered into treaty with the new Republic, and obtained the confirmation of the articles established by the treaty of 1819.

The Florida purchase cost the United States $6,489,768.

---

[1] Benton.   Thirty Years in the U. S. Senate, I, 16.

It added to the national and public domain 59,268 square miles.[1]

TEXAS ANNEXATION AND TEXAS CESSION.[2]

The annexation of the Republic of Texas in 1845 added to the national domain 376,123 square miles, or 240,718,720 acres, but nothing whatever to the public domain until after the Mexican War. Texas was originally claimed both by Spain and France. Spain claimed it before 1763. France never ceded to Texas the claim based upon discovery by La Salle in 1682, and upon actual colonization in 1685, at Matagorda Bay.[3] By the purchase of Louisiana in 1803, the United States acquired the French claim to Texas. In a letter to James Monroe, under the date of February 4, 1816, Mr. Jefferson wrote as follows : "On our acquisition of that country [meaning Louisiana] there was found in possession of the family of the late Governor Messier a most valuable and original MS. history of the settlement of Louisiana by the French, written by Bernard de la Harpe, a principal agent through the whole of it. It commences with the first permanent settlement of 1699 (that by De la Salle in 1684 having been broken up) and continues to 1723, and shows clearly the continual claim of France to the Province of Texas as far as the Rio Bravo (Rio Grande), and to all the waters running to the Mississippi, and how by the roguery of St. Denis, an agent of Crozat, the merchant to whom the colony was granted for ten years, the settlements of the Spaniards at Nacadoches, Adais, Assinays and Natchitoches, were fraudulently invited and connived at."[4] Thus the author of the treaty of 1803 firmly believed that Texas, as far as the Rio Grande, was included in the Province of

---

[1] Public Domain, 120.

[2] Von Holst. Constitutional History of the United States, 1828–1846, Chapter VII, and also *ibid.* 1846–1850, Chapter III.

[3] Public Domain, 120.

[4] Jefferson's Works, VI, 551.

Louisiana, and consequently came into the possession of the United States through its purchase. But by the purchase of Florida from Spain in 1819, the United States agreed to accept for its western boundary the present eastern boundary of the State of Texas, which was then acknowledged as a province under Spanish rule. This treaty of 1819 was regarded by some as "the cession of Texas,"[1] as well as the purchase of the Floridas. But it was "a temporary measure," and Texas was destined to become a member of the Union.

TEXAS AFTER THE MEXICAN INDEPENDENCE.

On February 24, 1821, Mexico, by the treaty of Cordova, obtained its independence; Texas and Coahuila became one of the States of the Mexican Republic. Meanwhile the tide of immigration began to roll into the United States. The number of immigrants increased rapidly after 1825. They preferred to settle on free soil, and went to the Northwest. The Southerners began then to cross the border of Mexico and to settle in Texas. They were slaveholders and land speculators.[2] In order to counteract the influence of the non-slaveholding States, the Southerners found themselves compelled to extend slave territory. The plains of Texas were good soil for the propagation of servile institutions. The Sabine River was but a nominal international boundary, for though Texas was under a new Mexican Government, it was dominated by the Anglo-Americans from the Southeastern States. These Texas settlers obtained large grants of land from the Mexican Government, under the pretence of being Roman Catholics.

From 1827 to 1829 attempts were made on the part of the United States to purchase Texas from the Republic of Mexico. In 1827 Mr. Clay, then Secretary of State in President Adams' cabinet, offered $1,000,000 for the cession of Texas,

---

[1] Benton. Thirty Years in the United States Senate, 15.

2. e.g. Stephen Austin !

but the offer was not formally tendered to the Mexican Government by the United States Minister, Mr. Poinsett. In 1829 Mr. Van Buren, Secretary of State under General Jackson, offered $5,000,000 for Texas, but Mexico refused the offer. She misapprehended the situation. It was foreordained that revolution was to sever Texas from the new Mexican Union. It was impossible to keep free, liberty-loving, adventurous Anglo-American settlers in Texas under a Latin, Roman Catholic domination in Mexico.

The colonization laws of Texas granted a league of land, equivalent to 4,604 acres, to each settler who was the head of a family. She also granted one-third of a league, or 1,476 acres, to each single man.[1] This liberal land policy induced adventurers from neighboring States to settle in Texas and to identify themselves with her people. In 1830 the Mexican Government issued orders forbidding any further emigration from the United States; but in 1833 the population of Texas had grown so large that she was able to call a convention, and to constitute herself a Mexican State independent of Coahuila.

The separation of Texas from Coahuila was but the first step toward complete independence of Spanish-Mexican rule. Antipathy of race and land speculations worked together and carried Texas into a revolutionary war. On November 1, 1835, a "general consultation" of all Texas was held at San Felipe de Austin. War already existed between Mexico and Texas. Hostilities opened on September 20, 1835, on the western bank of the Guadalupe River. On November 11 the "consultation" adopted the plan of a provisional government, and on the following day it elected Henry Smith Governor.

On March 1, 1836, a convention assembled at the town of Washington, on the Brazos River. In this the darkest period of their history, the Texans made a declaration of

---

[1] W. M. Gouge. Fiscal History of Texas, 22.

independence, adopted a constitution, and established a government, to act till the constitution could be brought into full operation.[1] David G. Burnett was made President. On April 21 the battle of San Jacinto was fought. General Houston, the Texan commander, with a force of seven hundred men, met Santa Anna, the Mexican President, who commanded five thousand troops, fresh from work of devastation in the region beyond the Rio Grande. But Santa Anna was defeated and made a prisoner of war. He acknowledged the independence of Texas and obtained release.

On October 3, 1836, the first Congress of Texas met at the town of Columbia, and, on the 22d, General Houston, the hero of San Jacinto, was formally installed as President of the new Republic. In March of the following year the United States acknowledged the independence of Texas. This diplomatic course was followed by England and other European powers.

Final Annexation of Texas.

In August, 1837, Texas made an application to the United States for admission into the Union, but was refused. Meanwhile Texas had sold off her public lands, the chief source of her revenue. Land speculators and Southern politicians became now the advocates of the Texas annexation. In 1843 the question evolved into a national issue. In 1844 Mr. Polk was selected as the Democratic candidate for President upon the platform of annexing Texas. In April of the same year Calhoun, then Secretary of State in President Tyler's Cabinet, concluded an annexation treaty with Texas, but it was rejected in the Senate by a vote of 35 to 16. The Southern States of the Union favored annexation, but the North opposed it. It was an issue between slavery and free soil. Annexation was spoken of by Southern politicians as

---

[1] W. M. Gouge. Fiscal History of Texas, 49.

"re-annexation," for they regarded Texas as having been ceded to Spain by the treaty of 1819. Opponents to annexation regarded it as a virtual declaration of war against Mexico, for, by admitting Texas into the Union, a large tract of disputed territory would be incorporated into the United States, and, moreover, Mexico did not consider the recognition of Texan independence by Santa Anna as binding upon her.

The questions involved in the annexation of Texas may be briefly summarized as follows :[1]

1. The constitutional power of the Federal Government to admit independent foreign States into the American Union.

2. The effect of such annexation, if constitutional, in relations between the United States, Mexico, and other foreign powers.

3. The effect of the annexation as an extension of the territory of the United States and upon their commercial interests.

4. The effect of the annexation upon slavery.

5. The effect of the annexation upon the Union.

It is impossible here to discuss in detail any of these points. Suffice it to say that the Texas annexation was one of the most significant events in the history of the territorial expansion of the United States.

The Congress of the United States passed, March 1, 1845, a joint resolution for the annexation of the Republic of Texas. On July 4, 1845, Texas assented to annexation. Section 2, Article II, of the resolution provided that Texas "shall retain all the vacant and unappropriated lands lying within its limits to be applied to the payments of the debts and liabilities of Texas, and the residue of said lands, after discharging said debts and liabilities, to be disposed of as

---

[1] Cf. a pamphlet entitled "Thoughts on the Proposed Annexation of Texas," by "T. S." First published in the New York *Evening Post*, under the signature of "Veto." New York, 1844.

said State may direct; but in no event are said debts and liabilities to become a charge upon the Government of the United States."[1] This was the most important clause. Thereby Texas retained all her public land, and guaranteed the United States against all claims on account of her State debts. But it was soon found necessary for the United States to assume certain Texan obligations, and to purchase from her a disputed territory.

FINANCIAL CONDITION OF TEXAS.

When Texas revolted against Mexico her finances were in a most deplorable condition. We can better illustrate the general fact by quoting a report of the General Council which assembled November 3, 1835, at San Felipe de Austin. It says : "We authorized a contract for a loan of one hundred thousand dollars of the citizens of New Orleans, and appointed T. F. McKinney an agent to repair to New Orleans, and to carry it into effect. Our finances arising from the receipt of dues for lands, as will appear on file in Mr. Gail Borden's report, marked F, which were in his hands, are fifty-eight dollars and thirty cents. This money has been exhausted, and an advance by the President of the Council of thirty-six dollars. There were also several hundred dollars in the hands of Mr. Money, the alcalde of the municipality of Austin. Upon this money several advances have been made by Mr. Cochran, and probably will nearly cover the amount of money in the alcalde's hands; as such, you may consider that at this moment the Council is out of funds."[2]

Thus the revolutionists in Texas undertook war with an empty chest. All they had was land. They pledged public lands and public revenue in payment for loans. In the annexation treaty, therefore, public lands were retained by Texas. But she was deprived of import duties, which were

---

[1] Public Domain, 122.

[2] W. M. Gouge. Fiscal History of Texas, 18.

an important source of public revenue.   The United States
Government was therefore under some obligation to compen-
sate Texas for this loss of economic resources in the discharge
of her public debts.

There was, moreover, a boundary question to be settled
between the United States and Texas.   Texas claimed all the
lands east of the Rio Grande which are now in the Territory
of New Mexico.   The people in New Mexico declared that
they were not in the jurisdiction of Texas.   During the
Mexican War, New Mexico was captured by General Kearney.
The United States had therefore the right of conquest over
that disputed territory, but Texas had a claim to at least a
part of the conquered land.

On September 9, 1850, the "Boundary Act"[1] was passed
by Congress.   It was an act proposing to Texas: 1. The
establishment of her northern and western boundaries; 2.
The relinquishment of all territory claimed by her beyond
the said boundaries, and of all claims upon the United
States; and 3. The organization of New Mexico as a new
territory.   The territory to be ceded by this act was situated
to the north of 30° 30' north latitude, west of the one
hundred and third meridian of longitude west from Green-
wich, and north of the thirty-second parallel of north latitude,
and to extend to the Rio Grande River.   In consideration of
this cession of territory, and the relinquishment of all claims
upon the United States, the act proposed to pay to Texas
$10,000,000 in bonds bearing five per cent. interest and
running for fourteen years.   This bargain was virtually a sale
of public lands by Texas to the United States, in order to
redeem old pledges to her creditors.   General Houston, who
was the Senator from Texas, said that "it was the best sale
ever made of land of a worthless quality and a disputable
title."[2]

Texas called a special session of the Legislature, and on

---

[1] Statutes at Large, Vol. IX, 446.

[2] Quoted by Gouge. Fiscal History of Texas, 180.

November 25, 1850, accepted the proposed Act of Congress. On December 13, 1850, the Act of September 9, 1850, became operative, and the territory came into the jurisdiction of the United States. The cession embraced an area of 96,707 square miles, and the entire cost, including principal and interest, amounted to $16,000,000.[1]

THE MEXICAN CESSIONS.

By the treaty of Guadalupe Hidalgo, February 2, 1848, the United States obtained a most valuable acquisition of territory from Mexico. This was one of the economic results of the Mexican War. We are not here concerned with the military history of that war. Neither can we enter into a discussion of the political questions therein involved. Suffice it to say, the incorporation of Texas was the main cause of the war. In the disputed territory between the Nueces and the Rio Grande Rivers occurred the first hostile collision between the two countries. It was alleged that American blood had been shed on American soil. Therefore, on May 13, 1846, Congress declared that "war existed by the act of Mexico."

POLICY OF THE POLK ADMINISTRATION.

From the beginning, the administration of President Polk did not enter seriously into war with Mexico. It believed that Mexico would be compelled to succumb by very weakness, and that war would soon terminate in a treaty accomplishing the political object of the United States—viz.: a cession of territory. The recall of Santa Anna from exile, his restoration to power in Mexico, and his supposed friendship for the United States, were secret springs relied upon by Polk's administration to secure speedy peace from Mexico. War was declared not for the sake of war, but for advan-

---

[1] Public Domain, 185.

tageous peace. Santa Anna, who was thought to be a peace-maker, proved to be a war-maker.

On April 15, 1845, Mr. Nicholas P. Trist was appointed by President Polk as Commissioner to Mexico. He was sent to Mexico to negotiate a treaty and to effect a purchase of territory. On November 10 of the same year, Mr. Buchanan, Secretary of State, instructed the United States Minister, Mr. Slidell, to offer the Mexican Government $5,000,000 for the cession of New Mexico; and for the cession of California, $25,000,000; and for the Bay and Harbor of San Francisco, $20,000,000;[1] together with the assumption by the United States of all claims against Mexico. Nothing resulted from this offer. As we have already seen, war was declared in May, 1846. General Taylor took the field. He captured Matamoras and Monterey. The battle at Buena Vista was fought and Santa Anna was compelled to retreat. On March 9, 1847, General Scott reached Vera Cruz. He marched inland and defeated Santa Anna at Cerro Gordo. The city of Mexico was at the mercy of the Americans. The downfall of Santa Anna followed the capture of the Mexican capital, and a new administration under the republican party, which abhorred Santa Anna, was inaugurated in Mexico.

Mr. Trist was still at his post, although recalled a long time before. He negotiated for a treaty with the new administration, and it was concluded at the city of Guadalupe Hidalgo on February 2, 1848. The United States Senate adopted the treaty with some amendments on March 10, 1848, by a vote of 38 to 14. The ratifications of the treaty were exchanged in the following May at the city of Mexico, when the United States paid over $3,000,000 cash, according to a provision made in the seventh article of the treaty.

Through this treaty New Mexico and Upper California were ceded to the United States, and the lower Rio Grande, from its

---

[1] Public Domain, 125.

mouth to the town El Paso, was made the boundary of Texas. In consideration of the acquisition made by the United States, it was agreed that she should pay to Mexico $15,000,000, and assume the claims of American citizens against Mexico to an amount not exceeding three and one-quarter millions of dollars. The area of territory obtained by this treaty was estimated at 522,568 square miles.[1]

GADSDEN PURCHASE.

On December 30, 1853, another cession of territory was made by Mexico to the United States. This is known as the "Gadsden Purchase." It was secured in order to define more definitely the boundary between the two republics. The area of territory acquired through this purchase was estimated at 45,535 square miles, and the purchase cost the United States $10,000,000.[2]

THE PURCHASE OF ALASKA.

We have now come to the last acquisition of territory by the United States—viz.: the purchase of Alaska. In this purchase there are two noteworthy features of difference from all former territorial acquisitions. They are 1. Isolation of territory; and 2. The mode of the purchase. The territories hitherto acquired formed contiguous parts of the national domain. But this was not the case with Russian America. It is separated from the United States by British America. It forms a territorial outpost in the extreme northwest of the North American Continent, and lies so close to Asia that it looks "as if America were extending a friendly hand." Again, in former acquisitions, negotiations succeeded only after years of labor by such American diplomats as Livingstone and Pinckney and Trist. In the Alaska purchase, the American Minister at St. Petersburg had little to do. Even

---

[1] Public Domain, 134.   [2] *Ibid.* 138.

statesmen at home like Mr. Sumner, who was then Chairman of the Committee on Foreign Affairs, knew of it only a few hours previous to the signing of the treaty by Mr. Seward and Baron Stoeckel. The negotiation was concluded very summarily, and in a business-like manner, by the two parties concerned. Mr. Clay, the American Minister to Russia, spoke of this transaction "as a brilliant achievement which adds so vast a territory to our Union, whose ports, whose mines, whose timber, whose furs, whose fisheries, are of untold value, and whose soil will produce many grains, even wheat, and will become hereafter the seat of a hardy white population."[1]

Perhaps the acquisition of Alaska has not yet been duly appreciated by the American people, except by residents along the Pacific Coast. It may some day prove good policy for the United States to form a continuous coast-line along the upper Pacific, and to extend their national domain, if not over the entire North American continent, at least to that new and extreme "Northwestern Territory" near the "Frozen Sea."

History of the Discovery of Alaska.

Let us briefly review the history of Alaska. Alaska was first discovered by Captain Behring in 1728. Its discovery was due to the enterprising spirit of Peter the Great, who desired to know whether or not Asia and America were one continuous continent. He ordered out an expedition, but died before seeing its results. Behring was sent out by the Empress Catharine, and sighted land as far north as 67° 30'. He fulfilled the primary purpose of his expedition in discovering that the two continents are separated by a narrow body of water, which now bears the name of Behring's Strait. A second expedition was sent out in 1741. On this voyage Behring discovered many of the Aleutian Islands. Thus the Russian title to the peninsula of Alaska was founded as early as 1728 by discovery and exploration. Subsequent expedi-

---

[1] Seward's Works, V, 25.

tions and settlements under the Russian Government confirmed the title. While France and Spain had to give way to the United States in Eastern America, the aggressive policy of Russia, inaugurated by the great Czar, planted her colonies in Northwestern America, but only to follow the same inevitable course as other colonizing powers in North America.

On the Atlantic side no single European power had made exclusive exploration or settlement of any part of the country. Spain, England, France, Portugal, Holland, and Sweden had each its representative discoverers and explorers. Their claims were often so conflicting that appeal to arms was sometimes necessary to settle disputes. On the Pacific side, also, Russia was not the only nation to send out exploring parties to the Northern Seas. Not to speak of exploration in the sixteenth century by Drake, and of his christening the country "New Albion" between 38° and 42° north, the Northern Pacific coasts were explored in the latter part of the eighteenth century by the Spaniards, the French, the English, and even by the Americans. The Spanish expedition went out in 1775, and it reached the land as far as 58° north. The French expedition sailed in 1786, and reached 36′ farther north than the Spanish. La Pérouse, who was at the head of the expedition, remarked of Sitka that "Nature seemed to have created at the extremity of America a port like that of Toulon, but vaster in plan and accommodations."[1] France, after losing her great colonies of Louisiana and Canada, still seemed not to have abandoned the colonial project in North America; but La Pérouse's expedition came to naught.

In 1790, the coast of British Columbia was discovered by Vancouver. Thus the entire Pacific Coast was made known. In the following year, the Oregon coast was explored in detail by the United States captain, Gray. The United States, on the ground of Gray's discovery, raised a claim to the coast as

---

[1] Sumner's Works, XI, 197.

far north as the Russian discovery, which claim was finally settled as 54° 40' north, in the treaty of 1824 between Russia and the United States. In the following year, Great Britain made a treaty with Russia and recognized the southern boundary of Russian Alaska as 54° 40' north; but she claimed the territory south of that parallel by virtue of Vancouver's discovery in 1790.

Thus the United States and Great Britain came in conflict on the Pacific Coast. The claim of the United States to the Oregon territory was based, first, upon the cession of Louisiana; second, upon the waiving of Spanish claims to it by the treaty of 1819; and third, upon the discovery of the territory by Captain Gray in May, 1791. After much dispute, a treaty was finally concluded between the two nations. It was known as the "Oregon Treaty," and was concluded at Washington in 1846. By this treaty the northern boundary of the United States was fixed as the parallel 49° north latitude, and they waived the claim to the territory between 49° and 54° 40' north. The territory beyond 54° 40' north was never disputed, and Russia remained in absolute possession of the same.

Negotiations for the Purchase of Alaska.

In 1859, Mr. Gwin, Senator from California, opened an unofficial correspondence for the cession of Alaska with the Russian Envoy at Washington. The equivalent for the proposed cession Mr. Gwin placed at $5,000,000. Prince Gortschakoff, when informed of the price, said that it was "an unequitable equivalent," but wanted to think more of the matter. Meanwhile, civil war broke out in the United States, and the subject of the Alaska purchase was dropped.

In 1866, the Legislature of Washington Territory sent a memorial to the President entitled "In Reference to the Cod and Other Fisheries." In this memorial that body argued the necessity of the United States acquiring the Russian territories in North America. In June of the following year, the charter of the Russian-American Company was to expire, but it was expected by its friends that it would be renewed. This company was organized in 1799, under a charter from the Emperor Paul. It had the power of administration throughout the whole region of Northwestern America. Its charter was renewed from year to year. The company had its headquarters at St. Petersburg, and was very much like the original London Company of England, or the more famous East India Company. Russian America was virtually the property of the Russian-American Company. But this company leased its franchise to the Hudson Bay Company, which had its headquarters at London, and did much business in Russian America, as elsewhere. Renewal of the charter of the Russian-American Company would of course be attended with the renewal of the lease to the Hudson Bay Company. This was regarded by the people on the Pacific Coast as a great disadvantage to the United States. They planned to organize a company to replace the Hudson Bay Company, but found no possible chance of rivalry unless the territory were acquired by the United States.

Mr. Cole, Senator from California, labored at Washington for the acquisition of the territory in the interest of the people on the Pacific Coast. Official negotiations were at last begun. Baron Stoeckel, on leaving St. Petersburg for Washington in February, 1867, received instructions regarding the cession from the Archduke Carlanem, the brother of the Czar. Therefore, on his arrival in Washington in March, the Russian Envoy entered into the formal negotiation with Secretary of State Seward. Seven million and two hundred thousand dollars were offered for the territory. On March 29, Baron Stoeckel received instructions by cable from his Government, and at 4 o'clock the following day the treaty was signed by the Baron and Mr. Seward. Very little correspondence took place between the two parties, and very little time was occupied in effecting the cession.

SUMNER ON THE PURCHASE OF ALASKA.

On April 9, 1867, Senator Sumner made a masterly speech on " The Cession of Russian America to the United States,"[1] and favored the ratification of the treaty. " The speech," said the Boston *Journal,* " is a monument of comprehensive research, and of skill in the collection and arrangement of facts."[2] The great orator from Massachusetts, in speaking of the benefits to the Pacific Slope, said, " The advantages have two aspects — one domestic and the other foreign. Not only does the treaty extend the coasting trade of California, Oregon, and Washington Territory, but it also extends the base of commerce with China and Japan."[3] Sumner furthermore said : " To unite the East of Asia with the West of America is the aspiration of commerce now as when the English navigator recorded his voyage." As to the extension of dominion which this treaty would secure to the United States, he uttered very significant, statesmanlike words. He said, " With increased size on the map, there is increased consciousness of strength, and the heart of the citizen throbs anew as he traces the extending line."[4]

Again, he considered the acquisition of Alaska not only an extension of dominion, but also an extension of republican institutions. And here he touched the future. Time alone can verify his predictions. He said, " The present treaty is a visible step in the occupation of the whole North American continent. As such it will be recognized by the world and accepted by the American people. But the treaty involves something more. We dismiss one other monarch from the continent. One by one they have retired — first France, then Spain, then France again, and now Russia ; all giving way to the absorbing unity declared in the national motto— *E Pluribus Unum.*"[5]

---

[1] Sumner's Works, XI, 186–349.

[2] *Ibid.* 184.

[3] *Ibid.* 218.

[4] *Ibid.* 221.

[5] *Ibid.* 223.

Finally, Mr. Sumner spoke of government, population, climate, vegetable products, minerals, furs, and fisheries in Alaska, and treated his subject so fully that a contemporary French writer well said: "All that is known on Russian America has just been presented in a speech abundant, erudite, eloquent, poetic, pronounced before the Congress of the United States by the great orator Charles Sumner."[1]

The Senate ratified the treaty by an almost unanimous vote. Baron Stoeckel, when parting with Mr. Sumner on the night of March 29, 1867, at the house of Mr. Seward, said to the Senator, "You will not fail us?" Mr. Sumner did not fail them. The ratifications were exchanged June 20, 1867, and Alaska came into the possession of the United States. Its area is estimated to be 577,390 square miles, and its cost $7,200,000. Congress has just passed a law for organizing a territorial government in Alaska. The land laws of the United States will no doubt also extend over Alaska, especially as the recent discovery of gold makes the Territory more valuable than ever.

Concluding Remarks on the Public Domain.

We have thus sketched the history of the formation of the public domain of the United States. We have seen how it has grown, and what important questions of both national and international character have been involved in its acquisition. The purchase of Alaska completed the formation of the present domain of the great republic. Public domain is only a part of the national domain. Wherever newly-acquired public lands were situated beyond or contiguous to old national boundaries, we find new ones established. The Southeastern, Southern, Western, and Northwestern boundaries of the national domain were determined by a series of treaties with foreign powers for cession and purchase, beginning with the purchase of Louisiana in 1803, and ending with the cession

---

[1] Sumner's Works, XI, 185.

of Alaska in 1867. The Northern boundary question involved serious negotiations with Great Britain. It required a series of treaties and commissions, and even arbitrations by European monarchs. It required ninety years for its final adjustment.

Let us, in conclusion, summarize and illustrate the growth of the public domain by the following table:

TABLE SHOWING THE GROWTH OF THE PUBLIC DOMAIN.

	Dates.	Square Miles.	Acres.	Cost.	Cost per Acre.
Cession by States.......	Mar. 1, 1781–Apr. 24, 1802	404,955.91	259,171,787	......	...
For Georgia only[1]......	Apr. 24, 1802	88,578.00	56,689,920	$ 6,200,000.00	.10$\frac{1}{9}$
Louisiana Purchase....	Apr. 30, 1803	1,182,752.00	756,961,280	27,267,621.98	.03$\frac{3}{5}$
East and West Florida	Feb. 22, 1819	59,268.00	37,931,520	6,489,768.00	.17$\frac{1}{10}$
Guadalupe Hidalgo....	Feb. 2, 1848	522,568.00	334,443,520	15,000,000.00	.04$\frac{1}{2}$
Texas Purchase..........	Nov. 25, 1850	101,767.00	65,130,880	16,000,000.00	.24$\frac{7}{12}$
Gadsden Purchase	Dec. 30, 1853	45,535.00	29,142,400	10,000,000.00	.34$\frac{3}{10}$
Alaska Purchase.........	Mar. 30, 1867	577,390.00	369,529,600	7,200,000.00	.01$\frac{18}{20}$
Total...............		2,894,235.91	1,852,310,987	$88,157,389.98	.04$\frac{3}{4}$

According to this table, the entire public domain embraces the area of 2,894,235.91 square miles. If we deduct from this the area of the State of Tennessee, 45,600 square miles, which formed but a nominal public domain, the actual area of the public domain remains 2,848,635.91 square miles. Again, the purchase-price is $88,157,389.98. But, actually, public lands cost more than this sum, for we must take into account two important items—viz.: 1. The assumption by the United States of claims of American citizens against foreign powers from whom she purchased territories; and 2. The price paid to the Indians for extinguishing their land titles. These items must be included in the original cost of the public domain. Still, again, if we consider the disposition of public lands from a purely business point of view, we must, of course, add to the original cost-price the expense

---

[1] Area included in above.

for administration, surveying, etc.; and we must, furthermore, compare expenses with the receipts accruing from the sale of public lands. This method will enable us to realize how much the public lands have cost the nation; what income the Government derives from land sales; and the exact financial status of the land question at a given time. Public lands are no longer held as a source of public revenue: the present spirit of the land laws is to grant to actual settlers lands for house and home, and agricultural improvements. The subject of economy in administering and justice in disposing of the public lands, or the public property of the people, should interest the statesman and the citizen as well as every student of economics. In the following chapters we propose to examine these themes.

II.

ADMINISTRATION OF THE PUBLIC DOMAIN.

The first step toward administration of the public domain was taken by the Continental Congress, October 10, 1780. Congress passed a resolution on that day that territories to be ceded to the United States "shall be disposed of for the common benefit of the United States, and be settled and formed into distinct, republican States, which shall become members of the Federal Union, and have the same rights of sovereignty, freedom and independence as the other States. . . . . That the said lands shall be granted or settled at such times and under such regulations as shall hereafter be agreed on by the United States in Congress assembled, or any nine or more of them."[1]

This resolution was the corner-stone of the territorial system of the United States. It laid the foundation of all subsequent territorial legislation. It was the fundamental constitution

---

[1] Journals of Congress, III, 535.

relating to national sovereignty over the public domain. By this resolution, new States were to be erected out of the public lands, and they were to be republican in their political institutions.   The United States perpetuated their union by an inseparable territorial bond.   The new States were to owe their birth and life to the whole United States, and not to any individual State.   They were to be colonies of the nation at large, in whose material interests all the States of the Union were to have a common concern.   The Western lands were a means of uniting loosely-confederated States upon a solid basis of national interest.

The resolution had two principal objects in view—viz. : 1. The final formation of Territories into distinct, republican States; and 2. The disposition of unappropriated lands by the National Government.   The ordinance of May 20, 1785, for ascertaining the mode of disposing of lands in the Western Territory, and the celebrated ordinance of July 13, 1787, for the government of the Northwestern Territory, were both developments of the above resolution.   The origin of administrative measures adopted by Congress we cannot trace earlier than this resolution of 1780.   It was the beginning of American public-land legislation.   It was the foundation upon which all subsequent resolutions and ordinances were built.

The resolution of September 6, 1780, is also very important. It was initiative to the land-cessions, but not to the administration of the public domain.   Each had a distinct function of its own.   That of September 6, 1780, led the way to cessions, but that of October 10, 1780, led to administration.

We have already seen that, as early as October 30, 1776, Maryland protested against the Virginia Constitution, which reasserted ancient charter rights to the Western lands, and urged Congress to consider those lands as a common stock, to be parcelled out at the proper time into convenient, free, and independent governments.   The four years' persistent efforts of Maryland, as well as the remonstrances of other smaller

States, finally resulted in the resolution of October 10, 1780, soon followed by various ordinances for the government and disposition of the Western lands. The War for Independence lasted seven years. The dispute over the Northwestern Territory took one year longer for its final settlement. The day the Virginia cession was accepted by Congress marks the day of settlement of the long-protracted controversy. It was a day also on which a committee was appointed to draft a plan for the temporary government of the Western Territory.

For the sake of convenience, we shall divide the administration of the public domain into two heads—viz.: 1. The Ordinance of 1787; and 2. The Organization of the General Land Office. The former provided a civil government of a temporary character under the authority of Congress in the Western Territory, and the latter furnished governmental machinery for the administration and disposition of the public lands.

The territorial government and the General Land Office are two separate civil organs. The former has nothing to do with the public lands situated within the territory of its jurisdiction. According to the land laws, the General Land Office, under a superior functionary, disposes of the public lands and grants patents, but it has no connection with the territorial government.

The entire public domain is therefore under the authority of the General Land Office so far as its settlements and land grants are concerned. The territorial government deals with a body politic, and performs all its necessary functions, legislative, administrative, and judicial, until it ceases to be a territorial government. A republican State with a republican Constitution is then erected under the sanction of Congress, and enjoys a free and independent sovereignty upon an equal footing with the other States. But we are here concerned with the territorial government. To understand this, we must take a brief survey of the history of the Ordinance of 1787.

ORDINANCE OF 1787.

The very same day Virginia ceded her claims to the North-western Territory—that is, on March 1, 1784—a committee consisting of Mr. Jefferson, of Virginia, Mr. Chase, of Maryland, and Mr. Howell, of Rhode Island, reported a plan for the temporary government of the Territory.[1]   On the 17th of the same month the report was recommitted, and on the 22d a new report was made.   The new report was substantially the same as the old, except that the highly-fanciful names previously given to new districts were now stricken out. The report, after some amendment, was finally adopted April 23, by a vote of ten States to one.   Two States, Delaware and Georgia, were not then represented.   Thus the report of the committee, of which Mr. Jefferson was the chairman, became law.   There was one important omission which we shall soon notice.   This law for the temporary government of the entire Western Territory, north and south, is known as the Ordinance of 1784.   It was a precursor of the Ordinance of 1787, and as such it has an historical interest.

Provisions of Jefferson's Ordinance.

Let us first notice the provisions of the ordinance as submitted by the committee on March 1.   The ordinance defined the boundaries of new States.   Each State was to comprise two degrees of latitude, beginning at 31° north and extending as far northward as the Lake of the Woods.   The territory adjoining the Mississippi was to be bounded by that river on the west, and on the east by the meridian that passes the lowest point of the rapids of the Ohio River.   The territory east of this meridian had the same for its western boundary, and for its eastern boundary the meridian of the western cape of the mouth of the Great Kanawha.

This division of the Territory, as was shown by Dr. Adams

---

[1] Public Domain, 147–149.

in his study on " Maryland's Influence upon Land Cessions to the United States,"[1] seems to have been first suggested by Washington, with whom the Committee on Indian Affairs consulted. The organization and settlement of the Western Territory were inseparably connected with the Indian policy of the United States, for the claims of the natives were not yet extinguished. This had to be done before any definite occupation could take place. Therefore, the report of Mr. Jefferson's committee expressly stated that " the territory ceded or to be ceded by individual States to the United States, *whenever the same shall have been purchased of the Indian inhabitants* and offered for sale by the United States, shall be formed into additional States." . . . . The Indian title of occupancy had to be purchased from the then hostile Indians. As to the best policy to be pursued by Congress, a committee consisting of Mr. Duane, Mr. Peters, Mr. Carroll, Mr. Hawkins, and Mr. Arthur Lee, made a report on October 15, 1783,[2] after conferring with the commander-in-chief.

Mr. Jefferson's territorial divisions were, therefore, an outcome of the Indian policy as first planned by George Washington. In the latter part of the ordinance, some fanciful names were given to the new States northwest of the Ohio. They were as follows: Sylvania, Michigania, Chersonesus, Assenisipia, Metropotamia, Illinoia, Saratoga, Washington, Polypotamia, and Pelisipia.[3]

The question might here be asked why Mr. Jefferson and the committee did not name the States to be erected southeast of the Ohio, for the ordinance comprised the entire Western Territory north and south of the Ohio. This can be explained by referring to the report of Mr. Duane's committee already mentioned. The committee recommended to Congress that

---

[1] See *ibid.* 42. Also Secret Journal of Congress, October 15, 1783, and Journal of Congress of the same date.

[2] Journals of Congress, IV, 294–296.

[3] St. Clair Papers, II, 604; Sparks's Life and Writings of Washington, IX, 48.

"it will be wise and necessary, as soon as circumstances shall permit, to erect a district of the Western Territory into a distinct government,".... and that "a committee be appointed to report a plan, consistent with the principles of the Confederation, for connecting with the Union by a temporary government the purchasers and inhabitants of the said district, until their number and circumstances shall entitle them to form a permanent constitution for themselves, and, as citizens of a free, sovereign and independent State, to be admitted to a representation in the Union."[1] It might safely be inferred that the appointment of Mr. Jefferson's committee was a direct outcome of the above recommendation, but the committee's report said at the outset that "their report will be confined to Indian affairs in the northern and middle departments, as they are confined by the acts of Congress of the 12th July, 1775, and to the settlement of the Western country, these subjects being, in the opinion of the committee, inseparably connected, and the committee not being possessed of materials which enable them to extend their views to the Southern district."[2] The Southern district here referred to evidently meant the territory to be ceded by the three Southern States. Jefferson's committee, which was created through the recommendation of this Indian Committee, had therefore laid particular stress upon the Northwestern Territory, although the ordinance itself was general in its application, as we have already seen.

In dividing the Northwestern Territory, Mr. Jefferson must have been governed by the resolution of Congress, October 10, 1780. The resolution said that "each State which shall be so formed shall contain a suitable extent of territory, not less than 100 nor more than 150 miles square, or as near thereto as circumstances will admit."[3] The area of the maximum allowance of 150 miles square will contain 22,500 square

---

[1] Journals of Congress, IV, 296.
[2] *Ibid.* 294.
[3] Journals of Congress, III, 535.

miles, and that of the ten States, each having 22,500 square miles, will be 225,000 square miles. The area of the State cessions in the Northwestern Territory is estimated at 265,-877.91 square miles.[1] Thus, Mr. Jefferson's plan of dividing the Territory into ten States was quite consistent with the resolution of Congress of 1780. Numerically, the extent allowed to each State came as near as could be expected by Congress.

Now let us proceed to other points in the ordinance. It provided that the settlers, under the authority of Congress, should be granted the right to establish a temporary government, adopt the constitution and laws of any one of the older States, and erect townships or counties for legislative purposes. There was no property-qualification required for the exercise of these political rights. Free males of full age had civic privileges. This temporary government had to continue until the population in the new State reached 20,000 free inhabitants, when a permanent constitution and government could be established. After the organization of a temporary government, the settlers could have a member in Congress as their representative, with a right to debate, but not to vote. But when they should have increased to the number of the inhabitants in the least populous original State, their delegates, with the assent of nine States, as required by the eleventh of the Articles of Confederation, could be admitted into Congress on an equal footing with the original States.

Besides the points enumerated, the ordinance contained some other features of great importance. They were the general principles upon which both the temporary and permanent governments had to be established. They were as follows: 1. The new States shall remain forever a part of the Union. 2. They shall be subject to the Articles of Confederation like the original States. 3. They shall bear a part of the debts contracted by the Federal Government. 4. Their

---

[1] Public Domain, 11.

governments must be republican, and shall admit no person as a citizen who holds any hereditary title. 5. After the year 1800 A. D., there shall be neither slavery nor involuntary servitude in any of the new States.

Such were the provisions of the ordinance as submitted by Mr. Jefferson and his committee on March 1, 1784. The ordinance was finally passed on April 23, 1784, with some omissions and some additions. The additions were that the States should not interfere with the primary disposal of the soil by the United States; that they should not tax lands which were the property of the United States; that they should not levy higher taxes on the lands of non-resident proprietors than on those of residents; finally, that the articles of the ordinance should be formed into a charter of compact, and should stand as fundamental constitutions between the thirteen original States and each of the new States, unalterable except by common assent. The omissions consisted in striking out clauses that gave fanciful names to the new States and assigned boundaries to each of them; that which referred to the hereditary title of citizens; and lastly, that which prohibited slavery after the year 1800.[1]

The slavery clause was stricken out on the motion of Mr. Spaight, of North Carolina. The six States, Massachusetts, Rhode Island, Connecticut, New Hampshire, New York, and Pennsylvania, stood for, and Maryland, Virginia, and South Carolina against, the clause. Mr. Spaight's own State was divided. The rest of the States—Georgia, Delaware, and New Jersey—were not represented. It lacked only one vote to pass this anti-slavery clause, the votes of seven States being necessary to carry any measure in the old Congress.

"The defeat of Mr. Jefferson's anti-slavery clause was regarded at the time as a great calamity," says Mr. W. F. Poole, of Chicago, in his excellent paper on the Ordinance of

---

[1] See, for the ordinance, Public Domain, 147–149; Cole's History of the Ordinance, 7–10; Bancroft's Constitutional History, I, 153–159; St. Clair Papers, II, 603–606.

1787; but he adds that " Northern men soon saw that it was a most fortunate circumstance; for if slavery had been allowed to get a foothold in the Territory for sixteen years, it could not have been abolished at the end of that period."[1] The defeat proved fortunate, indeed, because of the later ordinance that prohibited slavery at once and forever in the Northwest after the passage of the fundamental law.

The Nestor of American history, Mr. George Bancroft, says: "The design of Jefferson marks an era in the history of universal freedom."[2] But it proved an initial attempt, rather than actual accomplishment. Mr. Jefferson seems to have been fully conscious of the defeat of his anti-slavery clause. Two years afterward he said: " The voice of a single individual would have prevented this abominable crime from spreading itself over the new country.... Heaven will not always be silent; and the friends to the rights of human nature will in the end prevail."[3] This "single individual," the mover against the anti-slavery clause, was one whom Jefferson styled "a young fool." In his declining years Jefferson again referred to the Ordinance of 1784, and said: "My sentiments have been forty years before the public; although I shall not live to see them consummated, they will not die with me; but, living or dying, they will ever be in my most fervent prayer."[4] The dying statesman's sentiments, originally cherished in the prime of his manhood, were realized forty years after his death[5] by the "Thirteenth Amendment" of 1865, when the curse of slavery was removed forever by the constitutional law of the United States. Mr. Jefferson's Ordinance of 1784, shorn of its chief glory, the proscription of slavery, became a law of the land. Soon after its passage,

[1] W. F. Poole in North American Review, April, 1876, 238.

[2] Bancroft's Constitutional History, I, 156.

[3] Jefferson, IX, 276.

[4] Jefferson to Heaton, May 20, 1826; quoted in Bancroft's Constitutional History of United States, I, 158.

[5] Jefferson died July 4, 1826.

the author of the law left Congress for a mission abroad.
Jefferson's connection with the ordinance then ceased.

WASHINGTON ON TERRITORIAL GOVERNMENT.

The ordinance, however, was a dead letter. " No settlement of the Territory was made under it."[1] Washington was
early and always aware of the importance of developing the
Western country. Under the date of December 14, 1784, he
wrote to R. H. Lee as follows : " Nature has made such a
display of her bounty in those regions, that the more the
country is explored the more it will rise in estimation. The
spirit of emigration is great; people have got impatient; and
though you cannot stop the road, it is yet in your power to
mark the way."[2] Again, under the date of March 15, 1785,
Washington wrote to the same gentleman and argued that
Congress ought to point out the most advantageous mode of
seating lands in the Western Territory, in order that good
government might be administered. He says : " Progressive
seating is the only means by which this can be effected." He
suggested also that one State should be marked out instead
of ten, in order to avoid any sectional conflict in the West.[3]

We have already seen that Jefferson's plan of dividing the
Western Territory first came from the suggestions of Washington; but here we find him advocating the marking out of
one State instead of ten. This change of view might be
attributed to the defeat of Jefferson's anti-slavery clause, and
the probable change in political conditions of the Northern
and Southern States. Massachusetts abolished slavery in her
Constitution of 1780.[4] So did Pennsylvania. Connecticut
made a partial abolition in 1784. The Northern and Eastern

---

[1] Poole's Ordinance of 1787, North American Review, April, 1876, 288.

[2] Sparks, IX, 80–81.

[3] Quoted in Bancroft's Constitutional History of the United States, I, 177, from MS.

[4] Poore's Charters and Constitutions, Part I, 957.

States were thus abolishing slavery.   But if, according to the Ordinance of 1784, ten new States were to be erected in the Northwest, where slavery was not prohibited, the anti-slavery States of the North would lose their political vantage-ground with the recognition of numerous slave States in the West. It must have been to quiet political uneasiness in the minds of Northerners that Washington suggested the marking out of only one State.   Indeed, it would not be too much to say that this idea of Washington, leading to what he termed the "progressive seating" of Western lands, was another "pioneer thought" in relation to the Ordinance of 1787, wherein the entire Northwest was organized as a single Territory, to be gradually formed into States not less than three nor more than five.

Congress did not take any further initiative, nor did the settlers petition that body to form a temporary government in the Western Territory according to the Ordinance of 1784. Accordingly, no government was organized under that ordinance, and the great Northwest remained but a wilderness. The census taken sixteen years later, in 1800, shows that the entire Northwest then contained but 50,455 inhabitants, distributed as follows: Ohio, 45,365; Indiana, 2,517; Illinois, 2,458; and Wisconsin, 115.[1]   From the year 1800, Ohio showed a very rapid increase of population.   She doubled it in every two years throughout the succeeding decade.   But this great frontier State had only a few detached settlements at the time when the ordinance of Mr. Jefferson was passed. In fact, the entire Northwest, except at Kaskaskia, St. Vincent's, and neighboring villages, was the home of roving Indians and wild beasts.   The settlements named were mostly colonies from Canada and Louisiana, and the settlers were slaveholders, for slavery was established by the French laws of Louisiana.   Besides, the emigrants from Virginia who emigrated to the Northwest, after the capture of French

---

[1] Tenth Census: Population, Part I, 4.

military posts by Colonel George Rogers Clark, brought with them negro slaves from the Old Dominion. Governor Coles states that it was this knowledge of the actual existence of slavery in the Northwest that led Mr. Jefferson to a gradual abolition movement, rather than to a sudden prohibition of the evil.[1]

PRELIMINARY STEPS TOWARD THE ORDINANCE OF 1787.

We have seen that Washington was reminding Congress of its duties to the West. Timothy Pickering was also aware of the importance of the settlement of the Western country. He wrote a letter, under the date of March 8, 1785, to Rufus King, of Massachusetts, which became historical on account of the controversy concerning the authorship of the Ordinance of 1787. He wrote as follows: " Congress once made this important declaration: that all men are created equal; that they are endowed by their Creator with certain inalienable rights; that among these are life, liberty and the pursuit of happiness; and these truths were held to be self-evident. To suffer the continuance of slaves till they can gradually be emancipated, in States already overrun with them, may be pardonable, because unavoidable without hazarding greater evils; but to introduce them into countries where none now exist can never be forgiven. For God's sake, then, let one more effort be made to prevent so terrible a calamity! The fundamental constitutions for those States are yet liable to alterations, and this is probably the only time when the evil can certainly be prevented. It will be infinitely easier to prevent the evil at first than to eradicate it or check it in any future time."[2]

Pickering was informed of the course of public business in Congress by Gerry, a member of Massachusetts. He was aware that the Land Ordinance reported May 7, 1784, by

---

[1] Governor Coles' Ordinance of 1787, 16.
[2] Pickering's Life of Pickering, I, 509–510.

a committee of which Mr. Jefferson was chairman and Mr. Gerry a member, would be read a second time March 16, 1785, and thought it opportune to write the letter to King, who was Gerry's colleague.

Mr. King did not disappoint his correspondent, for he made a motion on March 16, 1785, seconded by Mr. Ellery, of Rhode Island, that the following proposition be committed : " That there shall be neither slavery nor involuntary servitude in any of the States described in the resolve of Congress of the 23d of April, 1784, otherwise than in punishment of crimes whereof the party shall have been personally guilty; and that this regulation shall be an article of compact, and remain a fundamental principle of the constitutions between the thirteen original States and each of the States described in the said resolve of the 23d of April, 1784."[1]   The motion was to commit the proposition to a committee of the whole House.   It was an attempt to restore to the Ordinance of 1784 its anti-slavery article, which was lost by the motion of a delegate from North Carolina.   On the question for commitment, eight States— New Hampshire, Massachusetts, Rhode Island, Connecticut, New York, New Jersey, Pennsylvania, and Maryland—voted in the affirmative, and three States—Virginia, North Carolina and South Carolina—in the negative.   Mr. Grayson, of Virginia, voted in the affirmative, but his vote was neutralized by those of his colleagues.   Neither Delaware nor Georgia was represented.   The proposition was referred to a committee, but it was never called up for action, nor ever alluded to again in Congress.

With the commitment of the proposition, Mr. King's connection with the anti-slavery question in the ordinance ceased, for although Mr. King, as chairman of the committee to whom the proposition was referred, made a report April 6, 1785, recommending a fugitive-slave law, as well as the

---

[1] Journals of Congress, IV, 481.

prohibition of slavery after 1800 in the Western Territory, " there is no evidence that it was ever again called up in that Congress."[1]

From the time Mr. King put the motion till the final passage of the Ordinance of 1787—that is, during the period of two years—the subject of the government of the Western Territory was frequently taken up and discussed. During the winter of 1786, Monroe traveled through the Northwest, and formed an opinion that it was advisable to divide the Territory into States—not less than three nor more than five— and on his return moved in Congress that the subject of the division of the Territory should be referred to a grand committee. On March 24, 1786,[2] the grand committee made a report, and recommended to repeal that part of the ordinance which referred to the division of the Territory, in order that Congress might divide the Territory according to its own discretion.

About this time Mr. Dane made a motion that a committee should be appointed to consider the form of a temporary government in the Western States. The motion was adopted, and a committee consisting of Mr. Monroe, of Virginia; Mr. Johnson, of Connecticut; Mr. King, of Massachusetts; Mr. Kean, of South Carolina, and Mr. Pinckney, of South Carolina, was appointed. On May 10, 1786, the committee submitted their report. " It asked the consent of Virginia to a division of the Territory into not less than two nor more than five States ; presented a plan for their temporary colonial government, and promised them admission into the Confederacy on the principle of the ordinance of Jefferson. Not one word was said of a restriction on slavery."[3] The report was recommitted, and was considered from time to time.

While Congress was considering the plan for the temporary government of the Northwest, a petition was presented from the

---

[1] Bancroft's Constitutional History of the United States, I, 180.

[2] Public Domain, 150.

[3] Bancroft's Constitutional History of the United States, II, 100.

inhabitants of the Kaskaskias for the organization of government in that district.   The petition was referred to a committee consisting of Mr. Monroe, Mr. King, Mr. Pinckney and Mr. Smith, who made a report August 24, 1786, and ordered " that the Secretary of Congress inform the inhabitants of the Kaskaskias that Congress have under their consideration the plan of a temporary government for the said district, and that its adoption will be no longer protracted than the importance of the subject and a due regard to their interest may require."[1]   The petition was probably the only one of the kind on record that was presented to Congress after the adoption of the Ordinance of 1784.

On September 19, 1786, a committee consisting of Mr. Johnson, of Connecticut; Mr. Pinckney, of South Carolina; Mr. Smith, of New York; Mr. Dane, of Massachusetts, and Mr. Henry, of Maryland, made a report on the plan of temporary government for new States.   In this committee, Mr. Henry, of Maryland, and Mr. Dane, of Massachusetts, were substitutes for Monroe and King, who were away from Congress.   On September 29th, the report was taken up for consideration, and a clause in the ordinance that referred to the administration of the oath was debated, but all further consideration of the ordinance was postponed.[2]

On the 26th of April, 1787, the same committee reported " an ordinance for the government of the Western Territory." On May 9th, it was read a second time.   A provision in the ordinance that admitted a new State into the Union after its population became equal to one-thirteenth part of the population of the thirteen original States, was stricken out.[3] The clause that referred to the representatives of the Territory was debated.[4]   The ordinance, as finally amended, was ordered to be transcribed, and the following day was assigned

---

[1] Journals of Congress, IV, 688-689.
[2] Journals of Congress, IV, 701-702.
[3] Bancroft's Constitutional History of the United States, II, 105.
[4] Journals of Congress, IV, 746.

for its third reading, but on that day it was postponed, and further progress was for a time arrested.

Thus far we have considered three ordinances: 1. The Ordinance of 1784, which was at this time still binding; 2. The Ordinance of May 10, 1786; 3. The Ordinance of April 26, 1787. The chairmen of the respective committees by whom these various ordinances were reported were, as we have already seen, Jefferson, Monroe, and Johnson. The provisions of the first two ordinances have already been given at some length. The text of Jefferson's ordinance is to be found in the volume called "Public Domain," 149. That of Monroe's is to be found in Volume V., 79 and following pages, of the "Journal of the Old Congress." The text of Johnson's ordinance, as it stood on May 10, 1787, for the third reading, and as it came down without amendment to the 9th of July, only five days before the passage of the final Ordinance of 1787, was first published by Peter Force in the *National Intelligencer* of August 26, 1847. It is reproduced in the "Public Domain," 150–153, and also in the "St. Clair Papers," II., 608–612.

The comparison of Johnson's ordinance with the Ordinance of 1787 shows that the former was quite unlike the latter. So far as the plan of the temporary government, the appointment of Governor, Secretary, and Judges, the organization of the General Assembly, etc., are concerned, both ordinances, indeed, agree, but the older ordinance contains nothing which makes the later ordinance so justly celebrated.

Peter Force was unable to solve the mystery attending the complete metamorphosis which an ordinance of no special legislative merit underwent in five legislative days. He thus expresses himself: "Such was the ordinance for the government of the Western Territory when it was ordered to a third reading on the 10th of May, 1787. It had then made no further progress in the development of those great principles for which it has since been distinguished as one of the greatest monuments of civil jurisprudence. It made no provision for the equal distribution of estates. It said nothing of extending the fundamental principles of civil and religious liberty; nothing of the rights of conscience, knowledge, or education. It did not contain the articles of compact which were to remain unaltered forever, unless by common consent."[1]

PROVISIONS OF THE ORDINANCE OF 1787.

We shall now proceed to the real and final Ordinance of 1787. We shall treat its passage and provisions, but reserve to a later part of this paper the discussion about its authorship. The " Journals of Congress " show that, from May 11 to July 4, Congress had no quorum, and consequently Johnson's ordinance, which would have passed to its third reading on May 10, was postponed, and received no further consideration till the month of July. On the ninth of that month, the ordinances were referred to a new committee. The committee consisted of Mr. Carrington, of Virginia; Mr. Dane, of Massachusetts; Mr. R. H. Lee, of Virginia; Mr. Kean, of South Carolina, and Mr. Smith, of New York. Among the members of the committee, Mr. Dane was in the previous committee which reported an ordinance on September 19, 1786, and also on April 26, 1787. Mr. Dane was the man who made a successful motion to appoint a committee in which Mr. Monroe, as chairman, reported an ordinance on May 10, 1786. Mr. Kean served on the committee of Monroe in the same year, but he was absent from the Congress during the summer, and his place was filled by Mr. Smith, of New York. Both Kean and Smith were put on the same committee, Kean taking the place of Pinckney, his colleague, who was on the former committee, and Smith holding his own place, which was originally that of a substitute for Kean. Mr. R. H. Lee was a new delegate from Virginia who took his seat in Congress on the 9th of July. Mr. Carrington, as well as

---

[1] Public Domain, 152.

Lee, was a new member of the committee. Thus, in the committee there were three Southerners and only two Northern men. The latter were old members of the committee, while the former were new members, although Mr. Kean once served on the committee of Mr. Johnson in 1786. The States which were then represented in Congress were three Northern States—Massachusetts, New York, and New Jersey—and four Southern States—Virginia, the two Carolinas, and Georgia, soon to be joined by Delaware. On the 11th of July, the committee made a report on the ordinance for the government of the territory of the United States northwest of the Ohio. On the twelfth the ordinance was read a second time, and on the thirteenth it was read a third time, and passed by the unanimous vote of the eight States then present in the Congress. The only delegate who voted in the negative was Mr. Yates, of New York, but his vote was neutralized by the combined vote of his two colleagues, Mr. Smith and Mr. Harney. Mr. Dane attributed the dissenting vote of Mr. Yates to lack of information upon the subject.

Since the Ordinance of 1787 is the most important legislative enactment that Congress has ever passed with regard to the public domain, we shall examine its provisions in some detail. The ordinance opened with a division of the Territory. It raised the territory northwest of the Ohio into one district, subject to a change into two districts at the discretion of Congress. The estates of persons dying intestate were to be divided among their heirs in equal parts. Thus gavelkind was instituted in place of primogeniture. As to the disposition of real estate, the ordinance was very liberal, placing no restrictions upon it. When of full age, the owners of estates could devise or bequeath by will in writing attested by three witnesses. The conveyance of estates was also very simple. It was by simple lease and release, or by bargain and sale. Conveyances were to be recorded by registers within one year of the transfer. Personal property could be transferred by mere delivery. Such were the general laws with regard to real and personal property.

The ordinance then fixed the terms of Governor and Secretary, who were to be appointed by Congress.   The commission
of the former was for three years, and that of the latter
for four years.   During the exercise of their office, both
Governor and Secretary had to possess a certain number of
acres of freehold estate in the territory.   Three judges were
also to be appointed by Congress.   They had to exercise a
common-law jurisdiction, and could continue in office during
good behavior.   They also must have a freehold estate like
other civil officers.   To the Governor and Judges the temporary enactment of civil and criminal laws was entrusted.
These laws were binding until the organization of the General
Assembly.   The Governor was to be commander-in-chief of
militia.   He could appoint and commission all officers below
the rank of general.   He had also to appoint magistrates in
counties and townships which were to be laid out in those
portions of the district in which Indian titles were already
extinguished.

The ordinance next considered the subject of representation
in the General Assembly.   When the population of the district should reach five thousand free male inhabitants of full
age, the settlers could return to the General Assembly one
representative for every five hundred, until the number of
representatives amounted to twenty-five.   After this, the
Legislature had to fix the number and proportion of representatives.   Citizenship of three years' standing, residence in the
district, and holding of two hundred acres of land in fee-simple,
were necessary qualifications for a representative.   The elector
of a representative must also have the property-qualification
of fifty acres of land.   He must be a citizen of the United
States, and a resident in the district; or, if not a citizen, then
two years' residence and the holding of sufficient landed
property would qualify him for an elector.   The term of representatives was fixed at two years.

Next in order came the organization of the General Assembly,
the manner of appointment of members of the Legislative

Council, and the authority and functions of the General
Assembly. The General Assembly was to consist of the
Governor, Legislative Council, and a House of Representatives.
The Legislative Council was to be of five members. The
members were to be nominated by the House of Representatives and appointed by Congress. Their commission continued for five years, and their property-qualification was
the same as that of representatives. The General Assembly
was authorized to make laws for the good government of the
district not repugnant to the principles and articles laid down
in the ordinance. All bills that passed both Houses of
Legislature needed the assent of the Governor to become laws
of the district. The Governor had the power to convene,
prorogue, and dissolve the General Assembly. The Governor
was required to take an oath before the President of Congress.
All other officers appointed by Congress took oath before the
Governor. The Legislature was authorized to elect a delegate
to Congress by joint ballot of both Houses, who had the right
of debating, but not of voting.

Such was the organization of the temporary government
for the Northwestern Territory. The provisions of the
ordinance were comprehensive, covering all necessary technicalities as to administration, legislature, and judiciary in the
new Territory. But such provisions related merely to the
routine business of government. There is nothing especially
remarkable in them. If the ordinance had ended here, it
would never have deserved the praises which have been
lavished upon it. But the ordinance, happily, did not
end here. It contained a Bill of Rights which has made
it world-famous. Here let the noble ordinance speak for
itself: "And for extending the fundamental principles of
civil and religious liberty, which form the basis whereon these
republics, their laws and constitutions, are erected, to fix and
establish those principles as the basis of all laws, constitutions
and governments which, forever hereafter, shall be formed in
the said Territory; to provide, also, for the establishment of

States and permanent government therein, and for their admission to a share in the Federal Councils on an equal footing with the original States, at as early periods as may be consistent with the general interest: *It is hereby ordained and declared, by the authority aforesaid*, that the following articles shall be considered as articles of compact between the original States and the people and States in the said Territory, and forever remain unalterable, unless by common consent."[1] Thus ends the preamble of this celebrated compact.

The articles are six in number, and are as follows: First, religious freedom was guaranteed, whether in worship or sentiment. Second, the benefits of the writ of *habeas corpus* and of trial by jury were secured to the settlers. Furthermore, by the second article, the representation in the Legislature was to be proportionate, and judicial proceedings must be in accordance with the common law. All persons were bailable, except in extraordinary cases. All fines were to be moderate, and no cruel punishments could be inflicted. No man was to be deprived of his liberty or property except by due process of law. Private contracts or engagements were never to be interfered with in any manner whatsoever. The third article says: "Religion, morality and knowledge being necessary to good government and the happiness of mankind, schools and the means of education shall forever be encouraged." Again, due regard must be paid to the property, rights, and liberty of the Indians. The fourth article states that the new States must forever remain a part of the United States of America, and subject to the Articles of Confederation. They were to pay a part of the Federal debts, and to contribute duly to the expenses of the Government. They could not interfere with the primary disposal of the soil by the Federal Government, neither could they tax lands which belonged to the United States. Non-resident proprietors were not to be taxed higher than residents. Finally, the navigable rivers leading into the

---

[1] Public Domain, 155.

Mississippi and St. Lawrence were declared common highways, and forever free to all the citizens of the United States.

The fifth article related to the division of the Territory into States, and the boundaries of such States. The Territory had to be divided into not less than three nor more than five States. When the new States had a population of 60,000 free inhabitants, they could be admitted by their delegates into Congress on an equal footing with the original States. Then they could form a permanent constitution and government in conformity to the principles contained in these articles.

The sixth and last article, which brought about so much controversy with regard to its authorship, was in the following language: "There shall be neither slavery nor involuntary servitude in the said Territory, otherwise than in the punishment of crimes whereof the party shall have been duly convicted. *Provided, always,* that any person escaping into the same, from whom labor or service is lawfully claimed in any one of the original States, such fugitive may be lawfully reclaimed, and conveyed to the person claiming his or her labor or service as aforesaid."[1]

EULOGIES ON THE ORDINANCE OF 1787.

Such were the provisions of the charter of compact in this celebrated Ordinance of 1787, which superseded the resolutions of April 23, 1784, known as Jefferson's Ordinance. The act of 1787 became the corner-stone of territorial governments in the Western Territory. Statesmen and public writers have been loud in their praises of this ordinance not so much because of theoretical principles embodied in the ordinance as from its practical merits and from results at once and forever beneficial to the interests of the whole Union. "We are accustomed,"

---

[1] The text of the ordinance may be found (1) in the Public Domain, 153–156; (2) in the St. Clair Papers, II, 612–618; (3) in the Journals of Congress, IV, 752–754; (4) in the Magazine of Western History, Nov. 1884, 56–59.

says Daniel Webster, "to praise the lawgivers of antiquity; we help to perpetuate the fame of Solon and Lycurgus; but I doubt whether one single law of any lawgiver, ancient or modern, has produced effects of more distinct, marked and lasting character than the Ordinance of 1787. We see its consequences at this moment, and we shall never cease to see them, perhaps, while the Ohio shall flow."[1] The words of Judge Timothy Walker are no less decided than those of his great contemporary. Judge Walker said, "Upon the surpassing excellence of this ordinance no language of panegyric would be extravagant. The Romans would have imagined some divine Egeria for its author. It approaches as nearly to absolute perfection as anything to be found in the legislation of mankind; for, after the experience of fifty years, it would perhaps be impossible to alter without marring it. In short, it is one of those matchless specimens of sagacious forecast which even the reckless spirit of innovation would not venture to assail. The emigrant knew beforehand that this was a land of the highest political as well as national promise, and, under the auspices of another Moses, he journeyed with confidence toward his new Canaan."[2]

Eminent constitutional writers like Judge Story[3] and Mr. Curtis are also among the admirers of the Ordinance of 1787. Here are the words of Mr. Curtis: "American legislation has never achieved anything more admirable as an internal government than this comprehensive scheme. Its provisions concerning the distribution of property, the principles of civil and religious liberty which it laid at the foundation of

---

[1] Webster's Works, III, 263.

[2] An address delivered at Cincinnati, December 23, 1837. Transactions Ohio Hist. and Phil. Society, I, Part II, 189. Quoted by Mr. W. F. Poole in North American Review, April, 1876, and in the St. Clair Papers, I, 118.

[3] Judge Story says, "The ordinance is remarkable for the brevity and exactness of its text, and for its masterly display of the fundamental principles of civil and religious liberty."—Story's Commentaries, III, 187.

the communities since established under its sway, and the efficient and simple organization by which it created the first machinery of civil society, are worthy of all the praise that has ever attended it. It was not a plan devised in the closet upon theoretical principles of abstract fitness. It is a constitution of government drawn by men who understood from experience the practical working of the principles which they undertook to embody. Those principles were, it is true, to be applied to a state of society not then formed, but they were taken from states of society in which they had been tried with success."[1] Again, Mr. Chase, late Chief Justice of the United States, in the introduction to the "Statutes of Ohio," said, "Never, probably, in the history of the world did a measure of legislation so accurately fulfil, and yet so mightily exceed, the anticipations of the legislators. The ordinance has well been described as having been a pillar of cloud by day and of fire by night in the settlement and government of the Northwestern States."[2]

Many similar eulogies on the ordinance and its framers might be cited, but we shall be content with one more quotation, and that from an eminent authority, whose praise of the ordinance is somewhat more definite and precise than any of the eulogistic opinions hitherto quoted. Mr. Joseph S. Wilson, late Commissioner of the General Land Office, says, "This noble statute [referring to Section II. of the ordinance] struck the key-note of our liberal system of land law not only in the States formed out of the public domain, but also in the older States. The doctrine of tenure is entirely exploded; it has no existence. Though the word may be used for the sake of convenience, the last vestige of feudal import has been torn from it. The individual title derived from the government involves the entire transfer of the ownership of the soil. It is purely allodial, with all the incidents pertaining to that title as substantial as in the infancy of Teutonic civilization.

---

[1] Curtis' Constitutional History of the United States, I, 306–307.
[2] See W. F. Poole in North American Review, April, 1876, 234.

359] The Land Question in the United States.   101

Following in the wake of this fundamental reform in our State land laws are several others which constitute appropriate corollaries. The statute of uses was never adopted in the public-land States, and hence the complex distinction between uses and trust has never embarrassed our jurisprudence. We have, however, adopted one of the methods of conveyance to which that statute gave rise—to wit, the method of bargain and sale. Feoffments, fines and recoveries are entirely dispensed with, as also livery of seisin and its consequences. A conveyance is completed by the execution and delivery of the deed. Entailment and perpetuities are barred by the statute, which renders void all limitations beyond persons in being and their immediate issue, and which provides that an estate tail shall become a fee-simple in the heirs of the first grantor. All joint interests in land are reduced to tenancies in common. Joint tenancies never had an existence, and coparceners are now on a footing of tenants in common. Real actions, with their multitudinous technicalities, never had an existence in our Western jurisprudence, though some of the fictions of this form of action were and are still tolerated in some localities—e. g., the allowance of fictitious parties to a suit. Ejectment is now the universal remedy, being the only action for the recovery of lands. Action by ejectment is limited to twenty-one years, but refractory tenants may be more speedily dispossessed by the action for forcible entry and detainer. A dispossessed claimant may, at the option of the ejector, either pay for the land or receive pay for the improvements. For waste the party is liable in simple damages and no more. A tenant in dower forfeits the place wasted. In the older States we see evidences of the reflex benefits of the land legislation of our public-land States."[1]

After quoting this able exposition, the Public Land Commission adds, "This great American charter contains the basic

---

[1] Land Office Report, 1870, 28–29.

propositions as to land tenures of the laws of the United States and of most of the States of the Confederation, and became and is the foundation of the same statutes in all the public-land States and Territories. Under its care and provisions the Central and Western States and Territories of the Union, and the States in the territory south of the river Ohio, have grown from weak and straggling settlements to mighty commonwealths and organizations containing more than 25,000,000 of people. The ordinance began with a wilderness. Its principles, embraced in existing laws, now govern in area and population the domain of an empire."[1]

Such are the opinions of eminent authorities on the Ordinance of 1787. Indeed, the ordinance is a grand monument to American statesmanship, and will forever tower among the works of Federal legislation.

CONSTITUTIONALITY OF THE ORDINANCE.

Before we enter into the subject of the authorship of the ordinance, one word must be said touching its constitutionality. The Articles of Confederation made no provision for erecting the Territory into new States, and for admitting them into the Union. Therefore, the ordinance which extended national sovereignty over the new Territory was an unauthorized act. But the ordinance was a necessary sequence of the resolution of October 10, 1780. Virginia and other States quit-claimed the Western Territory, reposing faith in Congress that such an ordinance as that of 1787 would be issued by Congress in conformity to the resolution. Therefore, the root of constitutionality primarily lies in the resolution and not in the ordinance.

Although no constitutional question as to the validity of the ordinance was ever raised in Congress, yet contemporary statesmen seem to have been aware of its legal defects.

---

[1] Public Domain, 159.

Madison thus speaks in the *Federalist:* "A very large proportion of the fund [referring to the Western Territory] has been already surrendered by individual States; and it may be expected that the remaining States will not persist in withholding similar proofs of their equity and generosity. We may calculate, therefore, that a rich and fertile soil of an area equal to the inhabited extent of the United States will soon become a national stock. Congress have assumed the administration of this stock. They have begun to make it productive. Congress have undertaken to do more: they have proceeded to form new States, to erect temporary governments, to appoint officers for them, and to prescribe the conditions on which such States shall be admitted into the . Confederacy. All this has been done, and done without the least color of constitutional authority. Yet no blame has been whispered, and no alarm has been sounded."[1]

That the public acquiesced in the ordinance was because of its necessity. The vital issues and common interests that were involved in governing the Western Territory on such a basis as the ordinance proposed were enough to justify it, in spite of its non-constitutionality. Congress could not have acted otherwise than to enact this fundamental law. The true function of an enlightened government is to do what the public interest (the *salus publica*) requires. "Government is derived from the living necessities and united interests of a people. The State does not rest upon compact or written constitutions. There is something more fundamental than delegated powers or chartered sovereignty. The State is grounded upon that community of material interests which arises from the *permanent* relation of a people to some fixed territory."[2]

The ordinance was legislation upon a national "community of material interests," and therefore found its

---

[1] The Federalist, No. XXXVIII, 42–43.
[2] H. B. Adams. Land Cessions, 49.

support in the economic foundation of the State. "The truth is," says Judge Story, "that the importance and even justice of the title to the public lands on the part of the Federal Government, and the additional security which it gave to the Union, overcame all scruples of the people as to its constitutional character."[1] This fact also illustrates the old truth that institutions are not made, but grow by historical processes. The living necessities of a body politic are the loftiest guiding principles of government. The *salus publica* will perpetually guide the history of society, in spite of written instruments. The unconstitutional Ordinance of 1787 has shaped the history of the entire Western Territory, because it was framed upon necessity and suited the needs of republican expansion. It fairly stood the test of seventy years, and, although then once repudiated in one of its most essential clauses, its principles have finally won a complete triumph.

AUTHORSHIP OF THE ORDINANCE.

The authorship of the Ordinance of 1787 has been much disputed ever since Webster made incidental reference to it in his first speech, January 20, 1830, on Foot's resolution concerning the Western lands. "At the foundation of the constitution of these new Northwestern States," said Webster, "lies the celebrated Ordinance of 1787. . . . That instrument was drawn by Nathan Dane, then and now a citizen of Massachusetts."[2] This statement was opposed by Mr. Benton and Mr. Hayne, who ascribed its authorship to Thomas Jefferson. The controversy then became an issue between sections — the North and the South. Webster not only ascribed the authorship of the ordinance to a Northern man, but its passage to Northern influence; "for," said he, "it

---

[1] Story's Commentaries, III, 187.
[2] Webster's Works, III, 263–264.

was carried by the North, and by the North alone." This
was a gross error, and was contradicted by the Southern
Senators. As we have already seen, the ordinance was /
carried chiefly by Southern votes. All the Southern States,
except Maryland, were then represented, while the North
was represented by only three States. Webster made some
other errors in the course of his speech, which were corrected
by Mr. Benton. But the Southern opponents of Mr. Webster
were also wrong in their attempt to eliminate Northern
elements from the ordinance, and in ascribing its authorship chiefly to Mr. Jefferson. As a matter of fact, the dispute
in the Senate brought no true light whatever upon the subject; and the authorship of the ordinance, if it was due to a
single individual, was left undiscovered for half a century.

The above controversy drew, however, a letter from Mr.
Nathan Dane, of Massachusetts, the only surviving member
of the committee who served in the old Congress in forming
a temporary government for the Western Territory in 1787.
His letter was a reply to Webster's inquiry about the origin
of the ordinance, and was dated March 26, 1830. It was
published by the Massachusetts Historical Society in its
" Proceedings," 1867–1869 (475–480). In this letter, Mr.
Dane strongly urges his claims to the authorship of the most
important parts of the ordinance. He considered Jefferson's
resolution of 1784 merely as an incipient plan, not at all
matured for practical legislation, while the final ordinance
was a completed system. He said that the ordinance, which
was so " totally different in size, in style, in form and principle," did not contain altogether twenty lines that were ·
taken from Jefferson's resolution, and that even these were
differently expressed. He then analyzed the ordinance and
divided it into three parts. The first part consisted of " the
titles to estates, real and personal, by deed, by will and by
descent; also personal, by delivery." These, he said, were
selected from the laws of Massachusetts, except that the
ordinance omitted the double share to the oldest son. The

second part consisted of preliminary measures for the temporary government of the Territory. "Neither these parts nor the titles," he says, were "in Jefferson's plan." In this Mr. Dane was somewhat mistaken. The titles, indeed, were not found in Jefferson's plan, as Mr. Dane truly says, but the temporary measures formed its chief bulk. The third part consisted of "the six fundamental articles of compact expressly made permanent and to endure forever." These permanent parts, Dane assured Webster, were his own original production. He had added them, as well as the titles, to the previous ordinance, which came down to the third reading on May 10, 1787. With regard to the slavery clause, Dane said: "I have, as you will see, ever been careful to give Mr. Jefferson and Mr. King their full credit in regard to it." But he said that since a slavery clause in his handwriting was found attached to the printed ordinance, it was also his work and not entirely theirs. He did not, however, claim originality for the anti-slavery clause, but what he did claim was authorship of the clauses touching contracts, Indian protection, religion, morality, knowledge and schools.

Mr. Dane's claims are quite sweeping, but there are some self-contradictory passages in his letter. He expressly states that the titles and the six articles were taken from the laws and Constitution of Massachusetts, but, at the same time, he claims originality for some parts of them. Conflicts of statement are still more apparent if we examine another letter, written by Mr. Dane under the date of May 12, 1831, addressed to J. H. Farnham, Secretary of the Indiana Historical Society, which letter was printed in the New York *Tribune* of July 18, 1875. He says: "It will be observed that Provisions 4, 5, 6, [which] some now view as oppressive to the West, were taken from Mr. Jefferson's plan." He admits that these three provisions were taken from Mr. Jefferson's plan, but in a letter to Webster he states that, "if any lawyer will critically examine the laws and constitutions of the

several States as they were in 1787, he will find the titles
and six articles were not to be found anywhere else so well
as in Massachusetts, and by one who, in '87, had been engaged
several years in revising her laws." Thus Mr. Dane implied
that he utilized the laws of Massachusetts for the ordinance,
and did not give credit to Mr. Jefferson for any important
parts of the ordinance except the anti-slavery clause, with
some modification.

Another testimony of importance to Mr. Dane's cause is
the letter addressed by him to Rufus King under the date of
July 16, 1787—a letter printed in the New York *Tribune* of
January 31, 1855.[1] In this letter, Mr. Dane states that
" when I drew the ordinance (which passed, a few words
excepted, as I originally formed it), I had no idea the States
would agree to the sixth article, prohibiting slavery, as only
Massachusetts, of the Eastern States, was present, and therefore omitted it in the draft; but, finding the House favorably
disposed on this subject, after we had completed the other
parts I moved the article, which was agreed to without
opposition." This quite agrees with what Dane wrote to
Webster concerning the anti-slavery clause. He stated that
he added the sixth article after the ordinance went into
print. This must be the reason why the anti-slavery clause
is found in his handwriting and attached to the printed
ordinance. This letter is the most important one of all, for
it was written only three days after the passage of the ordinance, and under no outside influence.

Thus we have three letters of Mr. Dane in which he
claimed, more or less directly, the credit of framing the Ordinance of 1787. They are: 1. A letter to Rufus King, July
16, 1787; 2. A letter to Daniel Webster, March 26, 1830;
3. A letter to J. H. Farnham, Secretary of the Indiana
Historical Society, May 12, 1831. Besides these letters,

---

[1] Bancroft's Constitutional History of the United States, II, 430; or
Spencer's History of the United States, II, 202–209.

Dane also stated his claims to the authorship of the Ordinance of 1787 in his "General Abridgment and Digest of American Laws," published in Boston, 1823-24.   In his letters to Webster and Farnham, Mr. Dane quoted several passages from the above work.   In fact, Mr. Dane's contemporaries must have derived their knowledge of the authorship of the ordinance from the statements he made in the seventh volume of his "Abridgment of American Laws," 389, 390. A writer in the *North American Review*, July, 1826, reviewed Mr. Dane's "Abridgment," and said that Mr. Dane was "the framer of the celebrated Ordinance of Congress of 1787 for the government of the territory of the United States northwest of the river Ohio—an admirable code of constitutional law by which the principles of free government were extended to an immense region, and its political and moral interests secured on a permanent basis.   One of its fundamental provisions—that there shall be neither slavery nor involuntary servitude in the said territory—prevented, by a wise foresight, a mass of evils and rendered that fine country the abode of industry, enterprise and freedom."[1]   The writer further says that, "in drafting this ordinance, Mr. Dane incorporated into it the cardinal preventive provisions against impairing the obligations of contracts by legislative acts."   Again, Judge Story, in a foot-note to page 130 of the third volume of his "Commentaries on the Constitution," says: "It is well known that the Ordinance of 1787 was drawn by the Hon. Nathan Dane, of Massachusetts, and adopted with scarcely a verbal alteration by Congress.   It is a noble and imperishable monument to his fame."   Mr. Dane, in his letter to Webster, referred to the statement of the reviewer of his "Abridgment of American Laws" in the *North American Review*, July, 1826, and also to that of Judge Story in his "Inaugural Address" (page 58), as a support of his claim to the authorship of the ordinance.

---

[1] North American Review, July, 1826, 40–41.

In 1847, Colonel Peter Force, of Washington, as we have already stated, printed in the *National Intelligencer*, of August 26, several ordinances relating to the Northwestern Territory, but he did not enter into any controversy concerning the authorship of the ordinance. He simply brought forward several new facts, and left the work of philosophizing upon them to other investigators. The valuable service which Colonel Force had contributed toward the solution of the true authorship of the ordinance was the publication of the ordinance which came down to the third reading on May 10, 1787. It was an entirely different ordinance from that of July 13, 1787. He did not explain, could not explain, how such complete changes were brought about, but he stated certain facts in the following words: "It appears that in five days it was passed through all the forms of legislation—the reference, the action of the committee, the report, the three several readings, the discussion and amendment by Congress, and the final passage."[1] These facts proved to be interesting data for the future settlement of the great problem of the authorship of the ordinance.

On June 9, 1856, Governor Coles read a paper before the Historical Society of Pennsylvania on "The History of the Ordinance of 1787." He was a native of Virginia, and private secretary to President Madison. He was Governor of Illinois from 1822 to 1826, and at the time he read his paper was a citizen of the Keystone State and a member of the Historical Society. Governor Coles ascribed the authorship of the ordinance to Mr. Jefferson. After comparing the difference in the provisions of the ordinance of Mr. Jefferson and those of 1787, and after affirming that Mr. Jefferson's anti-slavery clause was adopted by Congress in the Ordinance of 1787, "with no change except the omission of the postponement of its operation until 1800, and the introduction of the clause for the restoration of fugitive slaves,"[2]

---

[1] Public Domain, 152.
[2] Coles' History of the Ordinance of 1787, 15.

Governor Coles then adds that "some of the above particulars would not have been stated so fully but for a claim which has been made to the authorship of the ordinance on behalf of Nathan Dane, of Massachusetts. To show a misconception somewhere, and, in a word, the groundless character of this claim, it is only necessary to state that Mr. Dane took his seat in Congress for the first time on the 17th of November, 1785—more than eighteen months after the ordinance had been conceived and brought forth by its great author, and been adopted by Congress, with certain alterations, the principal one of which, on motion of Mr. King, had been in effect cancelled and the original provision restored nearly in the words of Mr. Jefferson, eight months before Mr. Dane took his seat in Congress."[1]

Governor Coles' errors are too evident to need any refutation. His explanation of the origin and history of the ordinance is also a hasty patchwork; but the history of the practical operation of the ordinance, which occupies more than half of his work, is very valuable, and shows that he was a strong anti-slavery man. The paper was written two years after the principles of the ordinance were repudiated in Congress, and he therefore wrote it in full anticipation of the dreadful calamity of civil war. His object seems, not chiefly to come to the support of Mr. Benton and Mr. Hayne in the matter of the questioned authorship—although he paid an appropriate tribute to Mr. Jefferson—but to show the wise provisions of the ordinance, under which the Western States have grown into a free and prosperous country. Mr. Benton, however, found a support for his cause in Governor Coles, and, in his "Thirty Years in the United States Senate," stated that he fully concurred with the statement of Governor Coles concerning the authorship of the Ordinance of 1787.

We have seen, thus far, that the names of Jefferson and Dane have been chiefly mentioned in connection with the

---

[1] Coles' History of the Ordinance of 1787, 15.

ordinance. The historic question lay between a Southern statesman and a Northern lawyer. In 1872, another name came before the public. It was the name of Dr. Manasseh Cutler. The Rev. Dr. Joseph F. Tuttle read passages from the journals of Dr. Cutler before the Historical Society of New Jersey on May 16, 1872. Dr. Tuttle briefly sketches the life of the Massachusetts divine as follows: " The Rev. Manasseh Cutler, LL.D., was born at Killingly, Conn., May 28, 1742. He was graduated at Yale College in 1765. He then studied law and was admitted to the bar. He removed to Edgartown, Martha's Vineyard, and began the practice of his profession. Not long afterward he determined to study theology, and was ordained September 11, 1771, and installed pastor of the Congregational church in Hamilton, then Ipswich Hamlet, Mass. He served as chaplain in the American Army, during two campaigns, in the War of the Revolution. In 1786, Dr. Cutler had become associated with a company (subsequently known as the Ohio Company), whose leading spirits were Revolutionary officers, for the purchase of land north of the Ohio. In June, 1787, he went to New York as the agent of the company to negotiate with the American Congress for the purchase of a large tract somewhere in the new country west of Pennsylvania and Virginia. With consummate tact he accomplished his mission, and made a contract for the purchase of over a million and a half acres at two-thirds of a dollar per acre. He kept a journal of his journey and his proceedings at New York, from which it appears that his plan could only be carried out by allowing some private parties to make an immense purchase of Western lands under the cover of the contract of the Ohio Company. The bargain included five millions of acres, one and a half millions of which were for the Ohio Company, and the remainder for the parties operating through him."[1] After giving extracts from the journals, Dr.

---

[1] Proceedings of New Jersey Historical Society, Second Series (1867-74), III, 75.

Tuttle continues : " I cannot bring myself to drop this part of Dr. Cutler's history without referring to two *facts*, as I fully believe them to be such. The ordinance to be submitted to Congress was placed in Dr. Cutler's hands for his examination, and his two grand suggestions were adopted. The first was the exclusion of slavery forever from the Northern Territory, and the second was the devotion of two entire townships of land for the endowment of a university, and Section Sixteen in every township of land and fractional township in that vast purchase for the purpose of schools. These two ideas, adopted by all the new States, made the Great West what it is."[1]

The object of Dr. Tuttle was to present passages from the journals of Dr. Cutler which referred to New Jersey, Pennsylvania, and Ohio in 1787–88. Therefore, the reverend doctor did not enter into discussion of the ordinance further than the above citations. But, in the history of the literature touching the authorship of the Ordinance of 1787, we find, for the first time, the name of Dr. Cutler connected with the ordinance. His relation to the ordinance, as well as to the Ohio Company, certainly needed a further and more careful investigation, in order to reach the long-desired end of the controversy over the authorship of the Ordinance of 1787. It is, indeed, a somewhat singular fact that the true authorship of the world-renowned ordinance was so long shrouded in mystery. But the mystery was soon to be removed by the hands of a careful investigator. The credit of solving this long-mooted question is due to Mr. William Frederic Poole, now of Chicago. He entirely exploded old notions upon the subject in an able article entitled " Dr. Cutler and the Ordinance of 1787,"·which was published in the *North American Review*, April, 1876.

The year 1876 was the centenary of American Independence, and it suggested various reviews by able writers on the prog-

---

[1] Proceedings of New Jersey Historical Society, Second Series (1867–74), III, 75.

ress of American politics, economics, education, law, religion, and other kindred matters, during the century. Among these articles is found Mr. Poole's valuable contribution to the history of the Ordinance of 1787. Mr. Poole went through all existing literature relating to the ordinance, and made a careful examination of all, especially of the journals of Dr. Cutler. The result of Mr. Poole's investigation showed that Dr. Cutler, while negotiating for the purchase of lands for the Ohio Company, was taken into the counsel of the committee who were framing the ordinance, and was asked to make remarks and propose amendments, which he did on the 10th of July, and that these remarks and amendments formed the moral bulwark of the ordinance. Mr. Poole further showed that the sudden change in the final ordinance from that form which came down to the third reading on May 10, is to be accounted for by the personal influence of Dr. Cutler in the shaping of the ordinance. He wished the government and laws of the new Territory adapted to the needs of emigrants from New England. Mr. Poole shows how the enactment of the ordinance was inseparably connected with the " Ohio purchase." He says : " The Ordinance of 1787 and the Ohio purchase were parts of one and the same transaction. The purchase *would* not have been made without the ordinance, and the ordinance *could* not have been enacted except as an essential condition of the purchase. Both were before Congress and under consideration at the same time. . . . The ordinance has hitherto been treated as an isolated piece of legislation, and as such it has been a marvel and an enigma. When considered together, every fact in the origin and passage of the ordinance is explained, and is found to be connected with the agency of Dr. Manasseh Cutler."[1] " The ordinance," he further says, " is a condensed abstract of the Massachusetts Constitution of 1780. . . . . The Ohio Company, organized in Massachusetts and mainly composed of Massachusetts men, was the party proposing to

[1] Poole in North American Review, April, 1876, 257.

purchase these lands. That these prospective emigrants should desire and claim the privilege of living under the laws and with the institutions they had cherished and helped to frame, was as natural and reasonable as that this boon should have been granted to them by Congress. There was no intention on the part of Congress, or of any member, of forming an ordinance on this basis until after Dr. Cutler had arrived in New York on the 5th of July. . . . . The new point of procedure having been fixed, the drafting of the ordinance was much a matter of clerical routine. The work was evidently turned over to Mr. Dane, he being the only member of the committee who was familiar with the Massachusetts Constitution."[1]

By this course of argument, Mr. Poole shows that it was Dr. Cutler who furnished the committee with suggestions as to the proper basis and best principles upon which to frame the ordinance. Thus the historic gap which Colonel Force could not fill was made full and satisfactory. In the centennial year, the mystery involved in the history of the ordinance was cleared away.

We shall not, however, do justice to the subject if we here part company with Mr. Poole's article. The interest created by Mr. Poole in Dr. Cutler has perhaps carried some of his readers a little too far, and made them under-estimate the service which others besides Dr. Cutler rendered in the formation of the ordinance. The editor of the "St. Clair Papers," Mr. William Henry Smith, says that Mr. Poole himself "gives too little consideration to the influence of others."[2] Dr. Adams, who reviewed the "St. Clair Papers," entertains the view that there were many authors. "The Ordinance of 1787, like all products of wise legislation, was created, not by one man or one section of country, but by the concurrent wisdom of many men, and by the unanimous vote of Congress. Jefferson and Dane; Pickering and King, of Massachusetts; Carrington and

---

[1] Poole in North American Review, April, 1876, 258.
[2] St. Clair Papers, I, 122.

Lee, of Virginia; Kean, of South Carolina, and Smith, of New York; the moral and educational interests of New England (represented by Dr. Cutler), the economic interests of the whole country (providing for its public debts by the sale of public lands), the 'private speculation' of 'many of the principal characters in America' (Cutler's diary), the personal popularity of St. Clair with the Southern party, which wished to reimburse the General for his Revolutionary losses by making him Governor of the Northwest—all these influences, and many more besides, entered into the formation and adoption of the Ordinance of 1787."[1]

Neither the friends of Dane nor those of Jefferson and Dr. Cutler can justly claim the sole authorship of the ordinance for their candidate. So many influences came into play, from Jefferson's first motion to the final passage of the ordinance, that it would be unjust to disregard them. Mr. Poole's enthusiasm for the shrewd and diplomatic New England clergyman has certainly carried many of his admirers away. In reality, Mr. Poole's views are perhaps not very far removed from those of Mr. W. H. Smith, who says: "Dr. Cutler organized the victory," and secured liberal principles in the ordinance.

The writer of this monograph thinks Mr. Poole did not deal quite fairly with Nathan Dane. He was somewhat severe in criticising Mr. Dane's style of writing as obscure and ragged. In fact, Dane's bad style was one of Mr. Poole's grounds for believing that the ordinance was not Mr. Dane's own production, although Mr. Poole admits that Mr. Dane may have performed the clerical work. Mr. Poole also casts rather

---

[1] Dr. H. B. Adams' review of the St. Clair Papers in *The Nation*, May 4, 1882.

Note.—I do not understand that Mr. Poole ever regarded Dr. Cutler as the actual author of the entire Ordinance of 1787. Mr. Poole has been misapprehended by some of his friends and critics. His main idea was that the clever parson, Dr. Cutler, in the interest of the Ohio Company, pushed a revised ordinance through Congress—an ordinance expressing both Virginia and New England ideas in a way satisfactory to all parties.—ED.

strong reflections on Dane's character, for he says Dane did not make any claim to the authorship of the ordinance during the lifetime of Dr. Cutler, or during that of any other person concerned in its formation. Dr. Cutler died July 23, 1823. Mr. Dane's "Abridgment" appeared from 1823–1829. In this work Dane set forth his claim to the authorship of the ordinance. It would be extremely unjust to the honor of that representative and codifier of Massachusetts law to assume that he purposely withheld his "Abridgment" until after Dr. Cutler's death. Such a thing is more than improbable. Besides, Mr. Dane, in his letter to Rufus King, written three days after the passage of the ordinance, expressly stated that he drew up the ordinance, and that it was accepted with only a slight alteration. Webster's speech shows that he held Mr. Dane in high esteem. As to his legal attainments, a contemporary writer says that the author of the "Abridgment" has honorably discharged that which "every man, according to Lord Coke, owes to his profession."

Again, Mr. Poole reflected perhaps rather too severely upon St. Clair, who is said to have been cool toward Dr. Cutler until the Governorship of the Territory was suggested for the former. This point was strongly contested by Mr. Smith in the "St. Clair Papers," and, following him, by Mr. William W. Williams, in his contribution of an article entitled "Arthur St. Clair and the Ordinance of 1787" to the *Magazine of Western History*, November, 1884. In spite of these criticisms, Mr. Poole's article remains the masterpiece upon the subject of the Ordinance of 1787.

Let us, in conclusion, say with Spencer, though with the addition of a few more names, that enough of enduring honor for each and all must forever be associated with the names of Dane and Jefferson, Pickering and King, Grayson and Smith, Monroe, Carrington, Lee, Kean, Johnson and Cutler, and perhaps others, for the part taken by each in the long, laborious, and eventful struggle which had so glorious a consummation in the ordinance, consecrating forever, by one

imprescriptible and unchangeable monument, the very heart
of this land to freedom, knowledge, and union.[1]

OPERATION OF THE ORDINANCE.

The first Governor of the Territory appointed under the
ordinance by the old Congress was St. Clair. William
Sargent, Dr. Cutler's partner, was appointed Secretary.
When the new Constitution took effect in 1789, the first
Congress passed an act recognizing the ordinance under the
new Constitution of the United States. On May 7, 1800,
the Territory was divided into two portions, and the western
portion became Indiana Territory. On November 29, 1802,
the eastern portion was admitted into the Union as the State
of Ohio. On January 11, 1805, Indiana Territory was
divided into two parts, and the northern central portion
became the Territory of Michigan. On February 3, 1809,
Indiana was again divided, and its western portion was
created into the Territory of Illinois. Indiana and Illinois
were admitted into the Union in 1816 and in 1818 respectively.
In 1836, the Territory of Wisconsin was formed out of the
western portion of the Territory of Michigan. Michigan
and Wisconsin were admitted into the Union in 1837 and in
1848 respectively. In authorizing the Territories to frame
State Constitutions for their admission into the Union,
Congress stipulated that the government should be republican and not repugnant to the Ordinance of the 13th of July,
1787, or to the fundamental compact between the original
States and the people and States of the territory northwest
of the river Ohio. So the principles of the ordinance entered
into the provisions of the State Constitution, and guided the
political life of those new commonwealths.

After the Ordinance of 1787 was adopted, attempts were
made from time to time by the people of the Territory of
Indiana to repeal or suspend the sixth article of the charter.

---

[1] Spencer's History of the United States, II, 209.

Petitions to that effect were often presented to Congress, but fortunately with no effect. In 1802, General Harrison, then Governor of the Indiana Territory, and afterward the President of the United States, took part in the effort to introduce slavery into the Territory. A memorial of the Governor and Territorial Legislature was laid before Congress. It was referred to a committee in the House of Representatives of which Mr. John Randolph was chairman. The committee reported against the introduction of slavery, and the report was accompanied by the following remarks: "The rapid population of the State of Ohio sufficiently evinces, in the opinion of your committee, that the labor of slaves is not necessary to promote the growth and settlement of colonies in that region; that this labor, demonstrably the dearest of any, can only be employed to advantage in the cultivation of products more valuable than any known to that quarter of the United States; that the committee deem it highly dangerous and inexpedient to impair a provision wisely calculated to promote the happiness and prosperity of the Northwestern country, and to give strength and security to that extensive frontier. In the salutary operation of this sagacious and benevolent restraint, it is believed that the inhabitants of Indiana will, at no distant day, find ample remuneration for a temporary privation of labor and of emigration."

Both the Senate and the House repeatedly refused the petitions of the inhabitants of Indiana Territory, and sanctioned the Ordinance of 1787. After the Territory was divided into two portions, the contest for slavery diminished in the eastern, or Indiana part, and finally Indiana became a non-slaveholding State in 1816. In Illinois the battle continued till after that State was admitted into the Union; but there also the anti-slavery party triumphed, and never admitted that accursed institution to corrupt the freedom and industry of a young State. The reason why the two States in their early history evinced a tendency to slaveholding was because of their proximity to slaveholding States, and the consequent influence of early settlers who either emigrated from the slaveholding States or were actually slave-owners before the passage of the ordinance, according to the French laws of Louisiana or the laws of the English colonies after 1763. In general, the case was quite different in Ohio. There, with local exceptions in some counties, the settlers were chiefly from the Northern and Eastern States. Connecticut had its " Western Reserve " in regions bordering Lake Erie. The Ohio Land Company had settlements on the Ohio and Muskingum Rivers. Referring to the settlement by the Ohio Company, which was principally a New England enterprise, and which was composed of men of high position and wealth, Washington said : " No colony in America was ever settled under such favorable auspices as that which has just commenced at the Muskingum. Information, property, and strength will be its characteristics. I know many of the settlers personally, and there never were men better calculated to promote the welfare of such a community."[1] " Before a year had passed by," says Bancroft, " free labor kept its sleepless watch on the Ohio."[2]

Besides these settlements, there were also colonies sent out by Symmes and his associates of New Jersey, that settled on the Ohio and the Miami Rivers. The ordinance was prepared for these settlers of non-slaveholding States in the North and East, and the settlers themselves naturally expected an abode for free and industrious men who would subdue Nature and overcome all obstacles for the sake of home and posterity. Ohio had a fair start, and sturdily supported the ordinance. Michigan and Wisconsin concurred with Ohio, and never permitted their virgin soil to be defiled by slavery. The provisions of the ordinance were extended to all the Territories north of 36° 30', and shaped the history and institutions of the great Northwest.

---

[1] Sparks, IX, 385.
[2] Bancroft's History of the Constitution, II, 117.

To the territory south of the Ohio River the provisions of the ordinance were extended by the Act of Congress, May 26, 1790; but the sixth article was discarded. When the "Missouri Compromise" was repealed in 1854, the ordinance, for a short period, sank into oblivion. Here let us quote from Governor Coles' "History of the Ordinance": "To a cool and dispassionate observer, who has a knowledge of the enlightened origin, the great popularity, and beneficial effects of the ordinance, it seems to be incredible that it should have been repealed, and especially denounced as violating the great principles on which our Government is founded. Yet such has been the fact; and what adds to the astonishment is, that this has been done by men professing to be of the Jefferson school of politics. . . . The wisdom, expediency and salutary practical effects of the ordinance could not be more clearly shown than by contrasting its operations with those of its substitute. Under the ordinance from 1787 to 1854, the Territories subject to it were quiet, happy and prosperous. Since its principles were repudiated in 1854, we have had nothing but contention, riots and threats, if not the awful realities of civil war. . . ."[1]

Indeed, the country experienced "the awful realities of civil war" not long after Governor Coles uttered these words; but the United States now enjoy peace, prosperity, freedom and steady economic growth. The wise and enlightened principles of the ordinance pervade the government and life of the people in the remaining Territories. When they grow in population to the required standard, they too will have State Constitutions, republican in form, and "not repugnant to the principles of the ordinance," and will be admitted into the Union. Then, and only then, will the great colonial and territorial dependencies of the United States in the West cease to exist.

---

[1] Coles, 32–33.

GENERAL LAND OFFICE.

The General Land Office is the Government-machinery through which the United States dispose of their public lands. It was instituted under the Treasury Department April 25, 1812, and was reorganized July 4, 1836.

Previous to the organization of the Land Office, Congress enacted from time to time various laws with regard to the disposition of public lands, and sold off portions through its agents. The Ordinance of May 20, 1785, created an office known as "the Geographer of the United States." Thomas Hutchins was the first-appointed Geographer. He had a number of surveyors under his direction. One was elected from each State. The Geographer was not, however, a negotiator of the public lands. His duty consisted chiefly in the supervision of surveys, and in the transmission to the Board of Treasury of the series of plats whenever the seven ranges of townships had been surveyed. The Treasury Board in turn transmitted these plats to the Commissioners of the Loan Office of the several States, who, after the execution of certain preliminaries, sold the lands at public vendue. Thus the Treasury Commissioners and the Loan Office Commissioners constituted administrative officers of the public domain, and sold out the surveyed lands in accordance with the ordinances of Congress.

HAMILTON'S PLAN FOR A LAND OFFICE.

When the new Constitution went into operation in 1789, and a new Congress had assembled, Mr. Scott, of Pennsylvania, argued the necessity of creating a General Land Office,[1] in order that the public lands might be disposed of to the best interest of the people, and especially of the pioneer settlers who had just begun to seek a home in the West. The

---

[1] Journals of Congress, IV, 520.
[2] Debates of Congress, I, 99–115.

need of parcelling out the lands in smaller lots than had hitherto been granted, and of granting them directly to actual settlers through agents of the General Land Office, was strongly emphasized by Mr. Scott and his followers, but their efforts bore no fruit.

The importance of the subject was not, however, overlooked by Congress. The House of Representatives called upon Alexander Hamilton, January 20, 1790, for suggestions respecting the best plan of disposing of the public lands. Hamilton transmitted his report to the House on July 20, 1790.[1] The report is said to have formed the basis for the future administration of the public lands. It concerns us here to see what was his idea as to the administrative organ of the public domain. Hamilton reported in favor of instituting a General Land Office at the seat of Congress. He argued this policy from a financial point of view. To institute the General Land Office was to realize the greatest returns from sales of the public lands. He also reported the advisability of opening district land offices for the accommodation of small purchasers.

The General Land Office was not, however, organized till twenty-two years later. But under the act of May 18, 1796,[2] the office of Surveyor-General was created, and in the following year General Putnam was appointed Surveyor-General of the Northwestern Territory. By the same act, the Secretary of the Treasury became the chief agent for disposing of the public lands. The act of May 10, 1810,[3] established district land offices in the Northwestern Territory, and they were placed under the charge of registers. Hitherto the Surveyor-General transmitted the plats of survey to the Secretary of the Treasury, but from this time forth he was to transmit them to the registers also. Besides the Register, the

---

[1] Public Domain, 198–200.
[2] Statutes at Large, I, 465.
[3] Public Domain, 201.

office of Receiver was instituted.   He was to receive money paid for the lands.

ESTABLISHMENT OF THE GENERAL LAND OFFICE.

On April 25, 1812, the General Land Office was instituted.[1] The new Commissioner was to perform those duties pertaining to the public lands which had hitherto been discharged by the Secretaries of Treasury and of War.   All returns relative to the public lands hitherto made to the Secretary of the Treasury were hereafter to be made to the Commissioner, and all patents were to be issued from his office.

At this time the General Land Office had charge of the cessions from various States and the whole of Louisiana.   Its administrative field was to expand more and more, according to the progress of surveys and new acquisitions of territory. Edward Tiffin, of Ohio, was appointed the first Commissioner.

In 1836, " an act to reorganize the General Land Office " was passed.[2]   The act provided for the creation of several new officers in the department.   They were as follows: Principal Clerk of the Public Lands; the Principal Clerk of Private Land Claims; the Principal Clerk of the Surveys; the Recorder of the General Land Office, and the Solicitor. The act further provided for the appointment of a Secretary by the President, whose duty was to sign for him all land patents.

In 1849 came another change in the General Land Office. Hitherto it had been a subordinate bureau in the Treasury Department.   The act of March 3, 1849,[3] created the Department of the Interior, whose Secretary, according to a provision of the act, was authorized to perform all duties in relation to the General Land Office—of supervision, appeal, etc.—

---

[1] Statutes at Large, II, 716.

[2] *Ibid.* V, 107.

[3] *Ibid.* IX, 207.

hitherto discharged by the Secretary of the Treasury. From that time the General Land Office has remained a subordinate bureau in the Department of the Interior.

As the superior officer of the Commissioner of the General Land Office, the Secretary of the Interior is allowed a certain amount of discretionary power in order that he may act with a certain degree of freedom, without being obliged always to go through legislative forms. He can discontinue the district land offices in any locality when he thinks their existence is no longer required. He has authority to order the departure from the regular rectangular surveys in the States where he thinks the system impracticable. The issue of military land patents; the appraisement and sale of reservations for town-sites; the adjustment of swamp-claims and claims to over-flowed lands with the Governors of the States interested; the calling of the Board of Equitable Adjudication for suspended entries of public lands and pre-emption claims; the designation of agricultural lands apart from mineral lands; the control of Yellowstone Park, and several other duties either of a routine or discretionary character, devolve upon the Secretary of the Interior. Finally, he must take the necessary measures for the completion of the public-land surveys.

RESPONSIBILITIES OF THE COMMISSIONER.

The existing laws thus require of the Secretary of the Interior the *supervision* of public business relating to the public lands, but the actual executive head of this important branch of public service is the Commissioner of the Land Office. It is this Commissioner who superintends all the machinery of the great Land Court of the country. It is he who chiefly disposes of innumerable cases of land claims. Upon him rests the responsibility of the faithful execution of the settlement laws. From him springs directly the title to land. Upon him depends the economic safety of the pioneer settler who struggles to create a home. He must fight with lawless land " grabbers." He must keep a watchful eye upon the condition of railroad corporations to which land grants have been made. Public interest requires him to avoid the introduction into the United States of English landlordism and other forms of land monopoly. These and all other such duties devolve upon the responsible office of the Commissioner of the General Land Office.

We shall now briefly inquire how the Land Office is managed under the direction of the Commissioner. In treating of the administration of the General Land Office, we shall divide the subject into two heads : 1. The General Land Office proper ; 2. The local offices subordinate to the General Land Office.

For the sake of conveniently carrying on practical administrative work, the General Land Office has created from time to time minor subordinate offices within itself. Each office is in charge of a chief clerk. At present there are twelve subdivisions—from Division A to Division P.[1] The entire force in the General Land Office, from the Commissioner down to the laborers, numbered 301 on June 30, 1883. Their compensation amounted to $383,000 per annum.[2]

The local subordinate officers are Surveyors-General and district land officers. At present there are sixteen surveying districts, each of which is under the charge of a Surveyor-General. These districts are Arizona, California, Colorado, Dakota, Florida, Idaho, Louisiana, Minnesota, Montana, Nebraska, Nevada, New Mexico, Oregon, Utah, Washington, and Wyoming.[3] The Surveyor-General is authorized to appoint his deputy to survey the public lands within his district. The cost of survey varies according to localities, but it cannot exceed the maximum fixed by act of Congress. The Surveyor-General makes contracts with his deputy under the approval of the Commissioner. The Surveyor's district

---

[1] Public Domain, 1230.
[2] *Ibid.* 553.
[3] *Ibid.* 554.

has no reference to the political divisions of the States, and is entirely conventional, depending upon the location of the public lands. When the survey of public lands within any particular surveying district is completed, then the Surveyor-General's office is closed and its archives are filed with the State Government.

Quite independent of surveying districts, the district land offices have been created for the accommodation of settlers. Since 1800 there have been created two hundred and fifty-eight district land offices, but there now remain only one hundred and five offices.[1] Each office is in charge of a Register and Receiver. The district land officers are agents for disposing of the public lands, and they come in direct contact with settlers. The execution of various settlement laws depends much upon the faithful discharge of the duties of these local officers.

In recent years efforts have been made to advance the General Land Office into a special department like the Department of Agriculture. In the first session of the Forty-Seventh Congress, the Committee on Public Lands, in the Senate, instituted investigations as to the actual condition of administration in the General Land Office. They reported a recommendation to create a Department of Public Lands. The Public Land Commission, which was created under the act of March 3, 1879, to codify the land laws of the United States, held the same view as did the Senatorial Committee. The late Commissioner, Mr. McFarland, repeatedly called the attention of Congress to the increasing work of the Land Office, and the lack of proper provision for the work.

We shall close this chapter by quoting words of the Public Land Commissioners, in their valuable work "Public Domain," with regard to. the importance of the General Land Office. "The General Land Office," says one Commissioner, "holds the records of title to the vast area known as

---

[1] Public Domain, 555.

the public domain, on which are hundreds of thousands of homes. Its records constitute the 'Domesday Book' of the public domain of the United States."[1] In the later edition of the work, the same Commissioner again says : " The General Land Office, charged with the care and custody of the public lands under the supervision of the Secretary of the Interior, is one of the most important and responsible public divisions in the administrative circles of the Government. The survey, sale or other disposition of the nation's public lands is within its control. . . . . Its jurisdiction reaches from Lake Erie to the Pacific Ocean, and from Canada to the Gulf of Mexico. Four-fifths of the lands of the entire area of the United States have been or are now under its supervision."[2] Public lands are a public trust. Recent investigations disclose shameful frauds and deceptions as prevailing in public-land entries.[3] The nation's interest demands a fair disposition of the public domain, and the importance of the office to which is entrusted the nation's property can hardly be exaggerated.

III.

LAND SYSTEM OF THE UNITED STATES.

The land system of the United States is of historical growth. It has passed through various legislative enactments, and through almost a century of practical administration. The present system has grown, perhaps, far beyond the anticipations of those who were first called upon to legislate concerning the public lands.

The chief object of the early legislators was to dispose of

---

[1] Public Domain, 166.

[2] Public Domain, 1222-1223.

[3] See in New York *Herald* a series of articles (April 6, 1886, and succeeding issues) upon such subjects as " Greedy Land Grabbers," " New Mexican Land Thieves," etc.

the lands as fast as they could, and with the proceeds to discharge public debts, to which the public lands were already pledged. Legislators did not look upon the public lands from the standpoint of settlement, but from that of finance. The Revolutionary War had wrecked the finances of the States. Commerce had faint life. Manufactures had not come into being. State contributions were often attended with technical difficulties. Loans accumulated, while credit was small. Continental paper was of little or no value. At this point of financial embarrassment, the most promising source of revenue was from the sale of Western lands, which became public domain through fierce political controversy. It is not strange, therefore, that early American financiers favored the passage of land laws which had revenue for their sole object. Public lands were then the common purse—the treasury of the nation.

EFFECT OF TERRITORIAL GROWTH.

While the question of revenue had so preponderating an influence, there came another influence which modified the land laws. It was the growth of the public domain. The legislators who deliberated on the public lands in the hall of Congress in Philadelphia, or in New York, had in view no broad Western horizon. Their outlook was limited to the lands lying west of the Alleghany Mountains and east of the Mississippi River. The lands which were pledged to public debts; the lands which were wrested from the British Crown; the lands which placed the Union on a solid basis of common interest; the lands which played the part of a centripetal force against the centrifugal tendencies of the States—these were the only lands which, in actual government and disposition, taxed the wisdom of the early legislators of the country. Beyond the Mississippi their views did not extend. They had no conception that the public agrarian trust was a growing one. They did not dream that the public lands would extend, within so short a time, not only beyond the Mississippi River, but even beyond the Rocky Mountains, beyond the Sierra Nevada, and finally down to the Pacific Coast. But such was the decree of fate. "America is a fortunate country," said Napoleon; "she grows by the follies of our European nations." True, Napoleon's own "follies" caused him to part with the vast imperial territory of Louisiana, and America grew to an enormous size. The original thirteen States almost trebled their domain. After the Louisiana Purchase, the public domain kept on growing, till the Czar of Russia ceded the peninsula of Alaska. So, finally, has arisen a vast agrarian empire of almost 3,000,000 square miles, which stands behind the original States like a territorial bulwark against any aggressive power beyond the Pacific.

The physical characteristics and natural conditions of this vast public domain are varied indeed. Some lands are subject to periodical floods. Some are now treeless deserts which need irrigation for successful culture. Some localities are valuable only for timber and stone. Some lands have coal and mineral deposits. Still others are particularly exposed to attacks from the Indians, and thereby need special protection to encourage settlement. Other lands, still, are covered with private land claims arising from grants by foreign powers. Again, as the public domain grew in size, certain lands had to be used, not only for purposes of settlement, but also for internal improvements, as well as for the advancement of education. These and many other facts and conditions had to be taken into consideration in the disposition of public lands. With the growth of the public domain, the land laws became very varied in different regions.

CHANGES IN PUBLIC SENTIMENT.

It was not merely the growth of the public domain that introduced variation in the early land laws of the country. Another potent factor in this process was the growth of public sentiment in regard to the ultimate disposition of the public lands. The old revenue idea gave place to the idea of actual settlement. The grant of homesteads for honest settlers became the spirit of the land laws.

In speaking of the waste lands in England, Edmund Burke said: "The principal revenue which I propose to draw from these uncultivated wastes is to spring from the improvement and population of the Kingdom. Throw them into the mass of private property, by which they will come, through the course of circulation and through the political secretions of the State, into well-regulated revenue." Such was the case with the wild lands of the United States. The nation had to derive wealth and strength from permanent material improvements upon the public lands by inviting enterprising settlers from the old States or from abroad, through free and liberal grants of land. The policy of land sales for the mere sake of revenue thus gave way to land grants for actual settlement.

This change in public sentiment was very gradual. It was the result of experience as well as of changed conditions. The sufferings of land purchasers under the credit system; the failure to realize any considerable revenue from cash sales; the increasing prosperity of the country from commerce and manufactures; the need of immigration of foreign-born citizens to occupy and develop the public lands—all these causes worked together to mould public opinion and shape the ultimate land policy of the United States.

Again, problems and motives of purely political concern often mingled with the land question. Not unfrequently party lines were drawn on agrarian issues. One party was instrumental in purchasing and acquiring new territories, while another enacted and executed land laws. The endless petitions and intrigues of speculators to secure special land grants hastened the enactment of a general land law in the form of the pre-emption act of 1841. In fact, the land laws of the United States developed from the actual needs of the people.

As is often the case with historical institutions, many early land laws have outlived their usefulness. They should be codified and reduced to a much simpler form, thereby remedying many incident evils. Experience will always show into what form the settlement laws of a country ought to drift. For historical illustration, let us now review the development of the land laws of the United States and see how they stand at the present time.

Military Bounties.

The earliest use which Congress had made of public lands was neither for revenue nor for settlement. It was for military bounties. " The primary use of focland, according to Bede's celebrated epistle to Egbert, was to reward soldiers."[1] So it was with the *focland* of the United States.

As early as August 14, 1776,[2] Congress promised a land bounty to British deserters, chiefly Hessian mercenaries. One month later, Congress passed an act promising land grants to officers and soldiers in the Continental Army. Through the prospect of land grants, Congress endeavored to enlist men in the army. This was the so-called " Continental Plan."

At this early stage of the Revolutionary War, Congress had little anticipation of the future constitutional controversy which conflicting bounty acts and the conflicting claims to the Western lands were instrumental in bringing about. Still less had Congress formed any idea what gigantic land corporations would eventually be called into existence by these same bounty acts. There was as yet no room for the consideration of conflicting claims to the Western settlements. Independence had just been declared. The war had only begun. The enlistment of soldiers on any plan which promised to secure a sufficient quota of troops was the one

---

[1] Henry Adams, Anglo-Saxon Law, 92.
[2] Laws of the United States (Duane Edition), I. 575.

thing needful. Accordingly Congress resorted to land bounties. The ways and means of fulfilling promises were for
subsequent consideration.

The land question cropped out in the Articles of Confederation. The ninth article provided that no State was to
be deprived of territory for the benefit of the United States.
Through this provision Congress recognized the claims of the
several States to their Western lands. This recognition
caused Maryland publicly to oppose the validity of such
claims—an opposition begun with the passage of the bounty
act of September 16, 1776.

The United States had at that time no public lands. How
was the Confederation to fulfill its promises? By purchasing
lands from individual States? Then the States, in their
collective capacity, would have to contribute money to buy
these bounty lands, and ultimately enrich such great landed
States as Virginia. Not only the money, but the very men
who were now fighting for the cause of liberty would sooner
or later find their way to the territory where the bounty
lands were to be allotted. The growth of the landed States,
both in wealth and population, was a necessary consequence
too obvious for calculation. Such an overgrowth of the
large States would both politically and economically pre-
ponderate over the small States. Maryland and other landless States would not be able to hold their own against such
an aggressive tendency on the part of the landed States.
Controversy over the land question was inevitable from the
very dawn of federal history, especially as the validity of
the claims to the Western lands could be questioned.

Thus arose at the dawn of the Republic's history a constitutional controversy on the disposition of unoccupied territory. The controversy continued several years, and ended in
cessions of land claims by the larger States. These cessions
gave birth to the public domain. It strengthened the Union,
and laid for it a lasting foundation. It created a common
federal interest and made valid the promise of the land
bounty.

While the question of the land cessions was yet pending, Congress passed a resolution that the ceded lands should be disposed of for the common benefit of the United States, and be settled or granted according to the manner agreed to in Congress. This was the first resolution as to the disposition of the Western lands. When New York ceded her claims, and Maryland signed the Articles of Confederation, Congress began to discuss modes of disposition, but nothing was determined till after the Virginia cession. The Virginia cession took place March 1, 1784, and on May 20, 1785,[1] Congress passed the first ordinance for ascertaining the mode of disposing of the Western lands.

GENESIS OF THE LAND SYSTEM.

This ordinance, the genesis of the land system, deserves examination in some detail. The ordinance instituted the so-called "Rectangular System" of surveys. According to this system, the Territory was to be divided into townships of six miles square by lines running due north and south, and by other lines crossing the first at right angles. The first line running north and south began on the river Ohio, at a point due north from the western termination of a line which was run as the southern boundary of the State of Pennsylvania. The first line running east and west of course started at the same point. The townships were designated by progressive numbers from south to north. Each range always began with No. 1, the ranges themselves being designated by progressive numbers from east to west. The townships were subdivided into sections of one mile square, or 640 acres, each township containing 36 sections, or 23,040 acres. This was the size of the normal township. In case natural hindrances made it necessary to have the survey of only a fractional part of the township, then the

---

[1] Journal of Congress, IV. 520, or Laws of the United States (Duane Edition), I. 563.

sections actually laid out bore the same numbers as if the township had been entire.   The actual size of such a township depended upon the extent of natural obstacles preventing the survey of an entire township.

RECTANGULAR SYSTEM OF SURVEY.

This rectangular system of survey has been established in the United States ever since the Ordinance of 1785.   Its merits have been recognized, and are well known.   Unfortunately, the origin of the system is not so well known.   The plan was first reported May 7, 1784, by a committee of which Mr. Jefferson was chairman.   The report recommended the division of the Western Territory into " hundreds," of ten geographical miles square, and these again to be subdivided into lots of one mile square.   As we have seen in the Ordinance of 1785, the size of the "hundreds" or townships was finally reduced to six miles square.   From what source the idea of dividing public lands into rectangular forms was first suggested to Mr. Jefferson and his colleagues is a matter of conjecture.   Mr. Donaldson, of the United States Land Commission, thinks that the natural features of the Western lands facilitated the work of longitudinal and latitudinal survey ; this, and the fact that Virginia in her deed of cession provided for the division of the Territory into States rectangular in form, not less than one hundred nor more than one hundred and fifty miles square, perhaps influenced Jefferson to recommend the rectangular system of survey.[1]   Professor Austin Scott, of Rutgers College, thinks that the idea was first suggested to Jefferson by De Witt, the Dutch surveyor, and that the system, imported from Holland, was primarily of Roman origin.[2]

Whatever may have been the origin of the system, it proved to be one of the best features of legislation respecting

---

[1] Public Domain, 178.

[2] The Rutgers Targum, December 12, 1884.

the public lands of the United States. Speaking of the merits of this system, Mr. Donaldson says : " Its recommendations to the public lie in its economy, simplicity and brevity of description in deeding the premises by patent and for future conveyancing, and in the convenience of reference from the most minute legal subdivision to the corners and lines of sections, and of townships of given principal base and meridians. Its greatest convenience is its extreme simplicity. . . . . It was originated for land-parcelling for sale, and it has answered the purpose."[1]   Again, General R. D. Mussey, of Washington, D. C., in a letter to Dr. H. B. Adams, of Johns Hopkins University, said : " I was specially interested in the history of the Ordinances of 1784 and 1787, and recalled the remark of a friend who had had a great deal to do with colonizing emigrants and others. He said that the rectangular method of land surveying was as great a conception in its way as any in that grand scheme for the management and disposal of the public lands. The ease, certainty and dispatch which this system has introduced into the determination of ' metes and bounds ' have been of incalculable advantage in promoting the settlement of the West. . . . . According to the ' Public Domain,' last edition, this plan had its origin in a committee of which Jefferson was a member, and presumably the idea was largely his. If so, it deserves to be ranked among the best of his contributions to the practical details of our Government machinery."   Indeed, the value of the rectangular system of surveys can hardly be overestimated. Not only does it afford positive advantages to the settlement, but, negatively, it prevents litigations, which are an inevitable consequence of irregular surveys and settlements.

METHOD OF SALE.

The Ordinance of 1785 established in detail a system of sale for the public lands. As soon as seven ranges of town-

---

[1] Public Domain, 188.

ships had been surveyed, the geographer had to transmit the plats to the Treasury Board. Thence the Secretary of War was authorized to take, by lot, plats for a number of townships equal to one seventh part of the entire number of townships contained in the seven ranges. This procedure was to satisfy the claims of soldiers to land bounties. Each time the geographer transmitted plats upon the survey of every seven ranges, the Secretary of War had to repeat the above procedure, until a sufficient quantity of land had been drawn to satisfy military grants. The remainder of the surveyed lands was drawn by the Treasury Board in the name of the thirteen States, according to their respective requisitions from the federal treasury. The board then transmitted a copy of the original plats of survey to the Commissioners of Loans in the several States, and notified them what townships had fallen by distribution to each particular State. The commissioners were authorized to advertise lands for the space of from two to six months, and then to sell them at public vendue in a manner prescribed by the ordinance.

The manner of disposing was to be as follows : Township No. 1 in the first range was sold entire, and No. 2 was sold only in sections, and so on alternately throughout the townships of the first range. Township No. 1 in the second range was sold by sections, and No. 2 entire, and so on throughout the second range. The third range was sold like the first, and the fourth range like the second, and thus alternately throughout all the ranges. The minimum price of land was one dollar per acre, not including the cost of survey, which was one dollar per section, or thirty-six dollars per township.

The ordinance further directed the reservation of Lot No. 16 in every township for the maintenance of public schools. This provision proved very beneficial to the cause of education.

This ordinance is significant in more than one respect. Not only did it institute the land system, but it respected

the promise of land bounties made to the officers and soldiers
of the Continental Army at the outbreak of the Revolution.
This promise the Government now proposed to fulfill through
the privilege given the Secretary of War of reserving bounty
lands before great tracts were put into the market.

But this provision was repealed July 9, 1788,[1] in consideration of a military reservation of a million acres which
was ordered by the resolution of October 22, 1787. The
proportionate distribution of lands to the several States, and
the subsequent sale by the Loan Commissioners in each State,
were alike found impracticable. The Treasury Board was,
however, authorized to select lands for sale.

Another significant feature in this Ordinance of 1785 was
the proposed sale of lands in an unlimited quantity above
the required minimum, which was an entire section of 640
acres. A rapid disposal of public lands and immediate
realization of revenue were greatly desired at the beginning
of the administration of the public land. "These Western
lands were looked upon by all the financiers of this period as
an asset to be cashed at once for payment of current expenses
of Government and extinguishment of the national debt."[2]
That this was the fact, can be judged from the tone of the resolution of April 29, 1784, which urged the cession of lands to
the States which still held them in suspension. It says that
"they [referring to the States] be urged to consider that, the
war being now brought to a happy termination by the personal
services of our soldiers, the supplies of property by our
citizens, and loans of money from them as well as from
foreigners, these several creditors have a right to expect
that funds shall be provided on which they may rely for
indemnification ; that Congress still consider vacant territory
as an important resource."[3]   By Act of March 3, 1795, " the

---

[1] Laws of the United States (Duane Edition), I. 569.
[2] Public Domain, 196.
[3] Journals of Congress, IV. 392.

net proceeds of the sales of lands belonging or which shall hereafter belong to the United States, in the Western Territory thereof,"[1] were constituted one of the six provisions that went to the "sinking fund."

With desire of immediate revenue, the Ordinance of 1785 allowed no credit for land purchases. Payments could be made either in specie or in loan-office certificates, reduced to a specie value on the then scale of depreciation, or by certificates of liquidated debts of the United States, including interest. In case immediate payment was not forthcoming, the lands were again to be offered for sale. In unfortunate contrast to this policy of immediate payments, the credit element was allowed to enter into the land system of 1787.[2] The resolution of April 21, in that year, required one third of the purchase-money to be immediately paid, but allowed three months' credit for the remaining two thirds. This was but another means to an economic end. It was to achieve the quickest possible sale of the public lands.

EARLY ATTEMPTS AT SETTLEMENT.

The settlement of the Western Territory, for which the Ordinance of 1785 was created, was not a novel idea. As early as 1742, the Ohio Company was organized in Virginia. Its object was to trade with the Indians and to settle the country. It secured a grant of several hundred thousand acres of land. Thomas Lee, Lawrence Washington, and other prominent Virginians, were the originators of this Ohio scheme. After the close of the French and Indian War, the subject of settlement received a fresh impulse from various sources. No less a personage than George Washington figured as one of the land speculators of the time.[3] In the *Maryland Journal*

---

[1] Statutes-at-Large, I. 435.

[2] Journals of Congress, IV. 739.

[3] See Washington's Interest in Western Lands, in Dr. Adams' paper on Land Cessions, University Studies, 3d Series, No. 1.

of August 20, 1773, Washington advertised 20,000 acres of land on the Ohio and Great Kanawha Rivers. About the same time the Walpole Grant was obtained through the personal influence of Benjamin Franklin. Several other land companies were started, some only in name, and others becoming afterward sources of litigation.

The Revolutionary War broke up every speculative scheme and checked every enterprise. Neither the Ohio Company nor the Walpole Grant was heard of again. But as soon as the war came to an end, individual settlers began to move toward the West. They began to trespass upon the public domain. They settled without title on unsurveyed lands. Thus they began to violate the fundamental provisions of the land system instituted in 1785, which required the extinguishment of Indian titles, and the survey of public lands before settlement. But these settlers were not very numerous. At the time the Ordinance of 1787 was passed, we find only a few scattered settlements on the Kaskaskias and at St. Vincent's, and a few French and Canadian villages.

OHIO COMPANY AND SYMMES' ASSOCIATES.

With the Ordinance of 1787 began active settlement in the Western Territory. The movement was inaugurated by the organization of the Ohio Land Company in 1786. The leading spirits of the company were General Rufus Putnam and General Benjamin Tupper. Both men were appointed surveyors under the Ordinance of 1785.[1] One night's friendly conference of the two veterans by a New England fireside resulted in a vast plan for colonization. The plan was accepted by the veterans of the Revolutionary Army, and such men as Winthrop Sargent, John Brooks, and Thomas Cushing joined the enterprise. The corporation was formally organized in Boston on March 3, 1786. It aimed to raise a fund to the amount of one million dollars in Conti-

---

[1] Journals of Congress, IV. 547.

nental certificates, and immediate steps were taken to collect subscriptions. But local discontent in New England from financial depression, and the consequent outbreak of Shay's Rebellion, retarded the progress of the company. In 1787, negotiations were opened with Congress for the purchase of lands in Ohio. Dr. Manasseh Cutler was then a special agent of the company.[1] We have already noticed the important service which the New England clergyman rendered in the passage of that celebrated ordinance. He succeeded also in effecting the purchase of lands for the Ohio Company. He and Winthrop Sargent, in behalf of the company, entered into a contract with the Board of Treasury, October 27, 1787, for the purchase of tracts of land on the Ohio and Scioto which were estimated to contain two million acres. At the conclusion of the contract, $500,000 of the purchase-money was to be paid down, but credit was given for the rest. The price was one dollar per acre, but a rebate to two thirds of a dollar was allowed under certain conditions. Rights to military bounties were recognized, acre for acre, in the payments of the company to the amount of one seventh of the entire purchase-money. Two sections in each township were granted for the support of schools and religion, and two entire townships for the founding of a university. Later, we find a donation of 100,000 acres to actual settlers within the purchase of the company. Originally, the contract stipulated for the purchase of 1,500,000 acres, but this amount was finally reduced to 964,285 acres, for which the company paid $642,856.66 in certificates and army land-warrants.[2]

Closely following the purchase made by the Ohio Company, John Cleves Symmes and his associates also bought a tract of land on the Ohio and Miami Rivers—a tract originally estimated to contain one million acres, but finally reduced to

---

[1] For the Ohio Company, see Poole's Ordinance of 1787 in *North American Review*, April, 1876. Also Alfred Mathews' Organization of the Ohio Land Company, *Magazine of Western History*, November, 1884.

[2] Laws of the United States, II. 277. See also Public Domain, 17.

248,540 acres. The terms of the purchase were the same as to the Ohio Company. The associates of Symmes were also Northern men. His petition was made " on behalf of the citizens of the United States westward of Connecticut."[1] Another contract for the sale of lands was made with the State of Pennsylvania in 1788. The tract now lies in Erie County, and is known as the " Erie Purchase."

Thus there were three large land-sales by Congress before the adoption of the system of disposing of lands through district land offices. Two of these purchases were made by private corporations of Northern men for the purpose of colonizing emigrants in the Western Territory. The same restless, enterprising, progressive spirit that had been the characteristic of the hardy Puritan settlers of New England, was manifested when they saw before them vast, fertile plains and primeval forests awaiting only the approach of labor and capital. New England society and institutions were reproduced in the Northwest, and they were destined to extend their influence from sea to sea.

HAMILTON'S PLAN FOR THE PUBLIC LANDS.

When Congress assembled in 1789, under the new Constitution, the subject of the public lands formed one of the most frequent topics of discussion. The House of Representatives soon called upon Alexander Hamilton for his views concerning the best plan of disposing of the public lands. On July 20, 1790, Hamilton made a report to Congress.[2]

This report was remarkable for its practical and financial suggestions. Hamilton thought that there would probably be three kinds of land purchases: First, by moneyed individuals and associations for the purpose of investment; second, by colonizing associations for the purpose of settling emigrants; and third, by unassociated persons either already inhabitants of the Western Territory or those who intended to emigrate

---

[1] Laws of the United States, I. 495.

[2] Public Domain, 198.

thither. Since the first two purchases already proposed
would be of such a character as to embrace a large quantity
of land, Hamilton thought that, from a financial point of
view, they required primary attention. But as the last
purchase was also an important one, he sought to harmonize
the interests of both large and small purchasers. For the
accommodation of the former class, he recommended the
opening of a General Land Office at the seat of Government where large contracts would mostly be negotiated by
interested parties, while for the benefit of the latter class he
recommended the establishment of local land offices where
small purchases could be made. Besides the commissioners in charge of these land offices, Hamilton suggested
the office of a Surveyor-General, with power of appointing a
Deputy Surveyor-General, as well as a number of Deputy
Surveyors.

Hamilton's suggestions as to the practical details in the
business of the Land Office were very characteristic of him.
While finance was to him a supreme interest, Hamilton did
not overlook the question of landed property. He seems to
have favored small land-holdings, for he made one hundred
acres the maximum quantity of an actual settler's holding.
But any quantity of land could be bought by special contract,
and two years' credit was allowed for the purchase of more
than a township of ten miles square—subject, however, to
certain conditions. Hamilton laid special stress upon the
financial value of the public lands. He deemed them one of
the foundations of his financial policy, for the certificates
issued for land on the public loan then proposed were allowed
to serve for warrants, and had to be received acre for acre in
payment for lands.

Important Features of the Land System.

Such was in substance Hamilton's plan for the disposition of the public lands. Some of the suggestions which
Hamilton made in his reports soon reappeared in acts of

Congress, notably in the Act of May 18, 1796.[1] This was
the first land ordinance which the new Congress passed since
its organization in 1789. There was nothing especially
original in it, for it was a modification of the Ordinance of
1785, with the embodiment of some of Hamilton's suggestions. The leading features of the old ordinance—*i. e.*, the
system of surveys, and the method of dividing land into
townships, and of subdividing the townships into sections; the
procedure of sale; the reservation of certain sections in each
township for specific purposes—were all retained in this act.
The creation of the office of a Surveyor-General, the formal
inauguration of a credit system, and the payment of certain
fees for certificates and patents, were things recommended by
Hamilton, and they were now made law by this act. The
price of land, instead of being reduced, as recommended by
Hamilton, was doubled, being now fixed at $2 per acre.

The next important change in the land system was introduced by the Act of May 10, 1800.[2] This act created the
office of Register and Receiver, whose duty was to take
charge of a land office. The act created in all four land
offices—one at Cincinnati, one at Chillicothe, one at Marietta,
and one at Steubenville. They were the first land offices
established by Congress. The present method of disposing
of public lands through district land offices began at this time.

Hitherto land had been sold in quarter townships and
sections. The above act ordered the Surveyor-General to
make further subdivisions of land—that is, into half sections.
In 1804, provision was made for the division of land into
quarter sections, and in 1820 the minimum quantity was
reduced to half-quarter sections; still later to quarter-quarter
sections—*i. e.*, 40 acres—which is the present minimum body
of land for sale.

Another important provision of the above act related to
the so-called "offered lands." Such lands as remained unsold

---

[1] Laws of the United States, II. 533.
[2] Statutes-at-Large, II. 73.

at the public vendue were subject to private sale at the then minimum price of $2 per acre. Some change was made in the mode of paying the purchase-money. Credit was allowed for four years. Payment could be made in four instalments, one fourth part of the purchase-money being paid each year. This method reduced considerably the revenue from public lands, the amount received in 1800 being only $443.75.[1] But, on the whole, this plan was an improvement upon the Act of 1796, and it was the first serious attempt toward the establishment of a general land system.

There intervened several decades between this time and the institution of a general pre-emption act. During this interval there were several important agrarian measures of both a general and a special character. During the first half of this period the purchase of Louisiana and Florida was effected. In 1805, a standing committee on public lands was appointed in the House of Representatives. In 1812, the General Land Office was organized. The public lands were now being rapidly settled, and several new States arose. Nothing is so remarkable as the rapid increase of population in the public-land States. In 1800, the entire Northwest contained only 50,000[2] inhabitants, the ratio of population being about one tenth to every square mile; while in 1840 the population had increased to 2,920,000, the ratio therefore increasing to about seven per square mile. In Ohio alone, from 1800 to 1810, the increase was nearly 409 per cent.

THE CREDIT FEATURE IN THE LAND SYSTEM.

The first forty years of the present century can be called the formative period of the general land system. The bitterest political controversy was connected with this period. As the struggle of the landed States in the old Congress had been to prevent the institution of the public lands, so now the struggle of the new landed States was to break up and

---

[1] Public Domain, 17.
[2] See Tenth Census of the United States—Population, Part I. 4.

appropriate the public lands within their own jurisdiction. To this period belongs one of the measures which instituted the so-called " American System " for internal improvement, and led the way to gigantic land grants which subsequently became sources of corruption and abuse. Again the country reached its most prosperous period, and the public debt was almost extinguished. As the surplus revenue is an economic problem in the United States to-day, so was it in this period of national history. Especially was it the case with the proceeds of public-land sales. Hence arose the question of distribution of proceeds, which for a time was carried by its friends.

During the early part of the present century, the land system presented one most discouraging feature. This was speculation in public lands. Speculation was an outcome of the credit feature in the land system. The Act[1] of 1800 provided : First, that every purchaser of public lands should pay toward surveying expenses six dollars for every section of land, and three dollars for every half section. Secondly, that the purchaser should deposit one-twentieth part of the purchase-money at the time of purchase, and one-quarter of the entire purchase-money, including the deposit, within forty days. A second quarter had to be paid within two years, a third quarter within three years, and the last quarter within four years after the day of purchase. Thirdly, that the purchaser should pay to the Register of the Land Office, when application was made, a fee of three dollars for every section and two dollars for every half section. Fourthly, that a fee of five dollars for patenting a section, and a fee of four dollars for patenting a half section, should also be required from every purchaser.

MOVEMENT OF POPULATION WESTWARD.

The terms of purchase provided by the Act of 1800 were very liberal, and offered sufficient inducement for enterpris-

---

[1] Statutes-at-Large, II. 73.

ing men to emigrate westward.   At this time, several States of the Union were making primary disposition of lands within their own boundaries.   Massachusetts was selling her lands in Maine; Connecticut, her "Western Reserve" in Ohio; Pennsylvania, her chartered lands through the State Land Office; while Virginia put into the market her lands in Kentucky; North Carolina, her lands in Tennessee; and Georgia, her lands in Alabama and Mississippi.[1]   The States offered their lands at a reduced price, so that Federal and State public lands came into open competition in the market.

The nineteenth century opened in America with the westward movement of population.   European nations were at that time involved in the Napoleonic wars; consequently, emigration from the Old World was small.   Prior to 1820, it has been estimated that the number of immigrants averaged about 8,000 persons per annum.[2]   It was not, therefore, emigrants from Europe that moved to the West at this particular period of American history, but rather emigrants from the eastern part of the United States.   Land could be obtained for an insignificant sum of money.   The terms were so liberal that settlers could pay the price of land with the first produce of their newly-broken farms.   Let us observe with how little money a settler could take up a section of 640 acres.   A cash payment of $331 was all that the settler needed in order to acquire this vast estate.   The charges were distributed as follows:

1. Register's fee for application, ...	$3 00
2. Expense for surveying, ...	6 00
3. One-twentieth of $1280, the price of a section at $2 per acre, to be deposited, . .	64 00
4. One-fourth of $1280, including deposit, paid within forty days after purchase, . .	256 00
5. Other small fees, ...	2 00
Total charges, . . .	$331 00

[1] Public Domain, 202.   [2] The American Almanac, 1884, 27.

As we have already seen, the other three-fourths ($960) of the purchase-money could be paid in three instalments, one each year, after the second year following the purchase, so that it required in all four years for the Government to realize the entire purchase-money. Any enterprising and industrious settler would be able to realize something from his newly-acquired land within two years of settlement, and thus find means for the payment of another fourth part of his indebtedness. At any rate, the agrarian inducements were so attractive to eastern farmers that a great exodus began to the Western Territory.

Speaking of the movement of settlers in the western part of New York, John Bach McMaster says: "They formed companies and bought millions of acres. They went singly, and purchased whole townships as fast as the surveyors could locate, buying on trust and selling for wheat, for lumber, for whatever the land could yield or the settler give."[1] In another place he says: " In 1800, the high-peaked wagons, with their white canvas covers, the little herd, the company of sturdy men and women, were to be seen travelling westward on all the highways from New England to Albany, and from Albany toward the Lakes. They were the true settlers, cleared the forests, bridged the streams, built up towns, cultivated the land and sent back to Albany and Troy the yield of their farms."[2] What was thus true of the western frontier of New York, was also true of the Ohio Valley. Restless immigrants kept constantly moving westward. Not all, however, were *bona-fide* settlers: some were land speculators, who bought real estate on credit with the hope of a future rise in value.

The credit system resulted in financial distress to many of the settlers. They became encumbered with debts to the Government, and the Government became the creditor of the distressed pioneers. On the 1st of October, 1808, the amount

---

[1] McMaster's History of the People of the United States, II. 573.
[2] *Ibid.* 574.

due the Government was estimated at $2,041,673.[1] Petitions were presented to Congress for the relief of the burdened settlers. It became necessary that relief should be granted in one way or another. On January 9, 1809, Mr. Morrow, of the Committee on Public Lands, reported to the House of Representatives in favor of the relief of land purchasers.[2] The committee first recommended the remission of interest. The Act of 1800 provided that a discount of eight per cent. should be allowed on the payments made before they became due, but also that six per cent. interest should be charged for the last three payments that were allowed to stand on credit. But the Act of March 26, 1804,[3] modified the above provisions. According to this act, no interest was to be charged for payments punctually made on the day they became due, but six per cent. interest was to be charged for all outstanding debts. It was the remission of this interest that the committee recommended. The committee also favored an extension of the time for completing payments. They reported that the general suspension of commerce prevented agricultural products from coming to market, thereby distressing farmers. The committee further urged an abolition of the credit system. They proposed to identify the interests of the settlers with those of the Government, and to prevent the accumulation of a large credit from increased sales, especially as at this time the lands owned by States and corporations were likely to become exhausted. The final recommendation of the committee was the reduction of price as a natural sequence of the abolition of credit.

ABOLITION OF THE CREDIT SYSTEM.

The result of the recommendations of the committee was an act, passed March 2, 1809,[4] which granted to the purchasers

---

[1] State Papers, Public Lands, I. 909.
[2] *Ibid.*
[3] Statutes-at-Large, II. 281.
[4] *Ibid.* 533.

of land an extension of two years for the completion of payments. This was the first relief act passed by Congress. It was speedily followed by other and similar acts. From 1809 to 1832 inclusive, no less than twenty-three relief acts were granted by the Government. They were either general or special in their application. By far the most important act was that of March 2, 1821. All other relief measures find their centre here. Previous to 1821 one act followed another, either extending the terms of payment, or suspending the sale or forfeiture of land for failure to complete payments. Such relief measures were only temporary, and could not effectually relieve the distress now spreading over the entire public domain. Neither could they eradicate the evil. Something more radical had to be done. The legislatures of the Territories often memorialized Congress for the relief of unfortunate settlers. The memorial of the Legislature of Indiana Territory which was presented to Congress under the date of September 21, 1814, shows in a measure that the settlers bought Government lands with the expectation of paying the cost out of the produce of the farms. The memorial says : " Many of the settlers have purchased their lands of the United States, and their last cent has in many instances been expended in making the first payment, under the impression that by means of their industry the produce of those very lands, together with the sale of surplus stock, would enable them to meet their respective balances as they would become due."[1]

The settlers were disappointed. Frontier life was often disturbed by outbreaks of Indians, and the settlers' farms remained unimproved for years. If the arrears on farms were not paid, the law had to take its course, and the lands reverted to the Government. To eject unfortunate settlers from their lands and log cabins must have seemed to the pioneers an inhuman thing. But the law had to be executed by Government representatives until relief came from Congress. Accordingly, one act after another was passed relieving the

---

[1] State Papers, Public Lands, II. 888.

pioneers of the West, as the **agrarian** laws of Rome relieved the suffering plebeians. But relief was endless unless the root of the evil was cut out. This root was the credit system. Congress became aware of the fact, and at last abolished the credit feature of the land system. This was done by the Act of April 24, 1820.[1] The act also reduced the price of land from $2 to $1.25 per acre, and thenceforward the duty of issuing proclamations for the sale of the public lands devolved upon the President of the United States.

CRAWFORD'S SYSTEM OF RELIEF.

The act prevented evils in the future, but did not altogether remedy those of the past. Cries for the relief of deep-seated distress did not stop. Mr. Crawford, then Secretary of the Treasury, recommended to Congress a plan which subsequently became law. This was the Act of March 2, 1821.[2] It was very comprehensive. Heretofore, relief had extended only to those who held land amounting to less than 640 acres, but this act extended the relief indiscriminately to all parties. It allowed all purchasers to relinquish their claims to the lands for which payment was not completed. The money could not be refunded by the United States, but could be credited for the lands men wished to retain. The act entirely remitted interest that had become due. It divided agrarian debtors into three classes. The first class were those who paid one-fourth of the purchase-money; the second class, those who paid one-half; and the third class, those who paid three-fourths. The first class of debtors were allowed to refund the balance in eight equal annual instalments; the second class in six years; and the third class in four years. The new debt or balance thus created had to bear an equal annual interest at the rate of six per cent., but the interest was to be remitted in case payments were made punctually

---

[1] Statutes-at-Large, III. 566.
[2] *Ibid.* 612.

at the time they became due. Such were the chief provisions
of the Act of 1821. They enabled settlers to consolidate
their holdings into such shape as their means would allow,
and at the same time put the Government, by receiving the
relinquished lands, into such a position as to be able to
execute that provision of the Act of March 3, 1820, which
authorized the President to sell the lands which had reverted
to the United States. Since the passage of the relief act of
1821, no less than ten similar measures were enacted. Most
of them followed the policy of the relief once established, and
extended the terms or allowed further contractions of holdings.
Under the credit system, the Government realized about
twenty-eight million dollars from the sale of about fourteen
million acres of the public lands.

POLITICS IN THE LAND QUESTION.

By the time the settlers' distress was relieved, the public
lands had developed another important matter for legislation,
and became the subject of much Congressional discussion.
One party supported one measure, and another party another
measure. Fierce political controversies raged from year to
year. Sectional issues often came to the front, and no little
ill-feeling existed between opposing factions. Constitutional
questions also were involved in the strife, and were discussed
pro and *con* by the ablest statesmen of the Republic—by
Webster, Clay, Calhoun, Benton, and others.

Never, perhaps, in the history of the public lands, was
Congressional warfare so fierce as at this time. The public
domain itself passed through a crisis. Had it not been for
the efforts of Webster and Clay, the unity of the public domain
would have been destroyed. Had the proposition triumphed
for retrocession, as advocated by Hayne and Calhoun, the
United States could not have had the uniform and general
land laws which the country has to-day. Again, the States
would have begun to compete with the Federal Government,

and would have invited unscrupulous speculators into the land market.

The State cessions which were proposed at this time were the direct reverse of the State cessions to the old Congress. The demand now was for the cession of the public lands to the new States in which they were situated. We have seen that the cession of the Western lands by Virginia and other States bound the Union together by ties of common interest. In the same way the preservation of the public domain at this period was instrumental in maintaining the Union.

The main issue was between Unionists and Separatists. Calhoun and his followers attempted to undermine the very foundation of the Union by securing retrocession of the public lands to the States. Webster upheld the cause of the Union, especially in that famous speech delivered in the Senate January 26, 1830, the second speech on Foot's Resolution.[1]

This remarkable controversy has a deep historical significance. Primarily, the matter was a reaction from various political measures. To effect a retrocession of public lands was to reduce the surplus revenue of the Federal Government. To reduce the surplus revenue was to check internal improvements and State distribution, as well as to suppress agitation in favor of freeing the blacks and colonizing Africa. The reaction was supported by deep-seated sectional ideas. The public-land policy was but a means to an end."

The controversy had fairly begun with Foot's Resolution. The resolution was to instruct the Committee on Public Lands to make inquiries as to the quantity of land still remaining in each State and Territory, and also to report as to the expediency of limiting for a certain period the sale of the public lands, except those already offered for sale, and then subject to private entry.[2] The resolution was originally inoffensive, but a few objectionable amendments and some

---

[1] Webster's Works, III. 270-347.
[2] Congressional Debates, VI. Part I. 11; or Webster's Works, III. 248.

remarks[1] on the resolution at once opened a field for discussion. We need not here examine in any detail the Webster-Benton-Hayne controversy; suffice it to say, Webster ably defended the national land policy. Webster's great speech, however, could not check the dispute; neither did it offer a solution to the vexed question.

APPEALS OF THE "LAND STATES."

During the two decades after the close of the second war with England the United States had increased steadily in wealth and population. The war of 1812 made the nation a debtor of over one hundred and twenty-seven million dollars, but in 1835 the debt was reduced almost to zero. At this period the public lands filled the treasury with their proceeds. In 1836, land revenue exceeded customs revenue by almost one and a half million dollars.

Again, immigrants had begun to pour in from Europe. In the decade from 1822 to 1832, their number increased almost tenfold. These immigrants became prosperous farmers by thrift and industry. Webster, speaking of the settler's prosperity, said: "Selection is no sooner made, cultivation is no sooner begun, and the first furrow turned, than he already finds himself a man of property."[2]

Such being the settler's good fortune, the public lands were fast taken up. The new States had no authority over the primary disposition of the lands; neither had they a right to tax them till after private ownership was established. Thus the Federal Government was ~~in one capacity~~ a great ~~landlord, and in another a great~~ untaxed proprietor.

When the public lands began to assume an important place in the economy of the nation, and when the legislators brought the land question into a political arena, the Western

---

[1] See Benton's Speech, Thirty Years in Congress, I. 131-134. See Hayne's Speech in Congressional Debates, VI. Part I. 43-58.

[2] Webster's Works, I. 352.

States, ever alert to their own interest, manifested a strong
desire to own the public lands. The legislatures of several
States presented memorials to Congress, and they were supported by the anti-tariff party. The legislatures petitioned for
the reduction of price as well as for the cession of the public
lands.

The whole question was referred to the Committee on
Manufactures, of which Mr. Clay was chairman. This was
out of the regular order, because the question had naturally
to go to the Committee on Public Lands. The reason why
the question was referred to Clay's committee is explained by
Clay's biographer, Mr. Colton. He says: "Mr. Clay being
a candidate for the Presidency in 1832, it was thought by his
political opponents that, by imposing on him the duty of
making a report on the land question, he would injure his
prospects in the western and new States. They believed that
he could not make a report on that subject consistent with his
known principles; and having a majority in the Senate, they
conspired to impose on him this duty, by referring the subject
to the Committee on Manufactures, of which Mr. Clay was
chairman. Mr. Clay and his friends protested against it,
but it was of no avail. . . . . The duty of preparing the
report, as was expected and intended, devolved on Mr. Clay.
Such is its origin."[1]

The report was presented to the Senate April 16, 1832.
It was a masterly piece of statesmanship, embodying sound
views as to the public lands. It deserves to go hand-in-hand
with Webster's great speech against Hayne.

Henry Clay fully understood the importance of the public
lands, and never, from presidential aspirations, yielded to
unscrupulous political schemes. He handled the subject
honestly, and boldly reported his recommendations. His
right conception of the subject may be judged from his
speech, in which he said: "No subject which had presented
itself to the present, or perhaps any preceding Congress, was

---

[1] Colton's Life and Times of Henry Clay, I. 460.

of greater magnitude than that of the public lands. There was another, indeed, which possessed a more exciting and absorbing interest, but the excitement was, happily, but temporary in its nature. Long after we shall cease to be agitated by the tariff, ages after our manufactures shall have acquired a stability and perfection which will enable them successfully to cope with the manufactures of any other country, the public lands will remain a subject of deep and enduring interest. In whatever view we contemplate them, there is no question of such vast importance."[1]

Clay's prophecy was correct: the tariff is no longer a burning political issue. But the public lands still remain, and form an important branch of administration. The American public is now indignant at the prevalence of systematic fraud and deception committed by unscrupulous land "grabbers." The popular cry is now for a reform of land laws. Again, in such a remote Territory as Alaska, the recent discovery of mineral resources has made that land an important acquisition, and will call the attention of the Government to the administration of that far-off Territory.[2]

We shall now briefly summarize the important points of Mr. Clay's report. After reviewing the history and origin as well as the sale of public lands down to 1832, the committee proceeded to inquire into the expediency of reducing the price of public lands. They said: "There is no more satisfactory criterion of the fairness of the price of an article than that arising from the briskness of the sales when it is offered in the market. On applying this rule, the conclusion would seem to be irresistible that the established price is not too high."

The committee then proved their position by showing, through statistics, the annual increase of the sales of the public lands during several preceding years. Another objection was that the reduction of the price was unjust toward

---

[1] Colton's Clay, I. 457–458.
[2] See President Cleveland's Message of 1885.

those who were already settled in the West. A further objection raised by the committee was that a reduction of the price would be attended by speculation. They said that "if the price were much reduced, the strongest incentives to the engrossment of better lands would be presented to large capitalists, and the emigrant, instead of being able to purchase from his own Government upon uniform and established conditions, might be compelled to give much higher and more fluctuating prices to the speculator." They cited as an example the military-bounty lands, which gave more benefits to the speculators than to those for whom the lands were intended.

Again, the committee considered that the reduction of the price would materially injure the interests of Ohio, Kentucky, and Tennessee, from which States, at this time, emigrants were moving to the West. If the price were reduced, the effect would be to depress the value of real estate in those States, as well as to drain them of their population and currency.

After the committee had refuted most conclusively the objections that the price retarded the sale, and that the price was a tax, they proceeded to the second branch of inquiry—respecting the cession of the public lands to the new States.

According to the estimate then made, the public lands consisted of more than one thousand and ninety million acres, which, at the minimum price of $1.25 per acre, represented the value of something over $1,362,500,000. Such being the case, the committee justly observed: "It is difficult to conceive a question of greater magnitude than that of relinquishing this immense amount of national property. If they were transferred to the new States, the subsequent disposition would be according to laws emanating from various legislative sources. Competition would probably arise between the new States, in the terms which they would offer to purchasers. Each State would be desirous of inviting the greatest number of emigrants, not only for the laudable purpose of populating rapidly its own territories, but with a view to the acquisition of funds to enable it to fulfill its engagements to the General Government. Collisions between the States would probably arise, and their injurious consequences may be imagined. A spirit of hazardous speculation would be engendered. Various schemes of the new States would be put afloat to sell or divide the public lands. Companies and combinations would be formed in this country, if not in foreign countries, presenting gigantic and tempting, but delusive, projects, and the history of legislation in some of the States of the Union admonishes us that a too-ready ear is sometimes given by a majority in a legislative assembly to such projects."

Another objection raised by the committee against the cession of the public lands was the new relation which from the transaction would arise between the General and State Governments.   The committee apprehended that among the debtor States a common feeling and a common interest distinct from the rest of the Union would inevitably arise. Again, delinquencies on the part of the debtor States would also inevitably arise, and these would result in the ~~relinquishment~~ *extension* of credit through endless petitions and varied manipulations, " or, if Congress attempted to enforce its payment, another and a worse alternative would be embraced." By the " alternative " was meant, probably, secession.   Here the committee struck the very root of the evil.[1]

CLAY'S DISTRIBUTION BILL.

Such were the views and considerations presented by the Committee on Manufactures with reference to the public lands. A bill accompanied the report, and was entitled " An act to appropriate for a limited time the proceeds of the sales of the public lands." This was the so-called " Distribution Bill." The Senate refused to take up the bill, and the subject was

---

[1] See Report in Colton's Clay, I. 453–460.

recommitted to the Committee on Public Lands. This committee made a counter-report about one month later.

Mr. Clay succeeded, however, in pushing his bill through the Senate. It passed the Senate at both the first and second sessions of the Twenty-Second Congress. But the concurrence of the House in the second session was secured only on the last day of the session, and it needed an immediate action of the President to make the bill a law. President Jackson retained the bill, "pocketed" it, as was said, and returned it with his objections at the opening of the Twenty-Third Congress. Thus the bill failed to become law.

In 1835, Clay again brought forward his Distribution Bill, which again passed the Senate, but was lost in the House. In 1841, the subject of the distribution was once more brought forward, this time as an administrative measure by which the incoming administration, under General Harrison, might make a point for itself as compared with the retiring administration of Van Buren. The bill was ably advocated by Webster and Crittenden. Here again constitutional questions were raised, and a critical examination was made of the conditions of cession to the old Congress. We cannot follow these manifold discussions; suffice it to say the distribution of the proceeds from the sale of the public lands was found to be neither unconstitutional nor impolitic. The bill finally became a law on September 4, 1841, and it provided that, after deducting ten per cent. of the net proceeds of the sales of the public lands within the States of Ohio, Indiana, Illinois, Alabama, Missouri, Louisiana, Arkansas, and Michigan, all the net proceeds subsequent to December 31, 1841, should be divided *pro rata* among the twenty-six States, and among the Territories of Wisconsin, Iowa, Florida, and the District of Columbia, according to their respective federal population as ascertained by the Sixth Census.[1]

With the distribution, so-called "State-selections," to the

---

[1] Statutes-at-Large, V. 453–458.

amount of 500,000 acres, were granted for the purpose of internal improvements to every new State that should be admitted into the Union. The act also extended the benefit to some of the new States already admitted. Thus the angry and deeply-agitating discussions growing out of the public lands, which had been raging with fury for the last ten or twelve years, were brought to a peaceful end.

PRE-EMPTION ACT.

By far the most important of all agrarian measures was the Pre-emption Act, which, incorporated with other measures, was passed September 4, 1841.[1] Neither the principle of distribution nor State-selections enter properly into the land system. They were simply the policy of the Government. They did not originate from the necessities of agrarian administration, but were simply the measures of one political party as opposed to another. The Pre-emption Act, on the contrary, was an integral part of the land system. It was the consummation of various land laws. It is still a law of the nation, though it has long outlived its usefulness. We shall now briefly consider the history, origin, and operations of the pre-emption law.

HISTORY OF THE PRE-EMPTION LAW.

" Pre-emption is a premium in favor of, and condition for, making permanent settlement and a home. It is a preference for actual tilling and residing upon a piece of land."[2] Pre-emption originated in the necessities of the settlers. It is not a free grant of land, but a privilege granted to a settler in purchasing a tract of land as against competitors. It amounts simply to the exclusion of competition, and the purchase of land at a minimum or double-minimum price, as the case may require.

---

[1] Statutes-at-Large, V. 453–458.
[2] Public Domain, 214.

The first pre-emption act was passed March 3, 1801.[1] It was a special act, and referred only to a handful of settlers within Symmes' purchase on the Miami River. Symmes' grand scheme of colonization had met with somewhat of a failure, and he was obliged to contract the area of his purchase. The non-fulfilment of conditions agreed upon with the United States entailed a forfeiture of at least a portion of his lands. Trouble ensued for the settlers. On account of the above forfeiture, the title of certain lands which the settlers had bought from Symmes became void. The settlers, aware of this fact, presented petitions to Congress, and sought recognition of their title. They argued that they were *bona-fide* purchasers and settlers; that they had paid Symmes for their holdings, and were unable to purchase a second time from the United States; that they believed their title was valid; that the rise of the price of real estate in their settlements was due to improvements which the settlers had made, and accordingly the price of land, if it must be demanded by the United States, should be reduced to the original rate—that is, to two-thirds of a dollar per acre instead of two dollars. Numerous petitions of this character were presented to Congress from time to time. Mr. Bruce, member of a committee to whom the petitions were referred, made a report, April 16, 1800, recommending that Symmes should be allowed to pay for the forfeited lands and complete his title, so that the settlers might not be disturbed.[2] But the Pre-emption Act of 1801 did not consider the financial relations between Symmes and his purchasers: it simply gave them the right to purchase holdings from the United States at the established price, and according to the Land Ordinance of 1800.

From this time till the passage of the general pre-emption act in 1841, no less than eighteen pre-emption acts were passed. Most of them were of a special character. Some

---

[1] Statutes-at-Large, II. 112.

[2] State Papers, Public Lands, I. 104–106.

referred to certain individual settlers in particular Territories, while others referred to the Territories or States themselves. //

Pre-emption was often a relief-measure for occupiers of the public lands. Such was the case with settlers or "squatters" in some of the Southern States; for example, Louisiana, Missouri, Arkansas, Alabama, Mississippi, and Florida. Immigrants came to those States with the expectation of securing public lands immediately after their arrival; but to their disappointment they found that public lands were not offered for sale in the sections where they wished to settle. The poor immigrants had no alternative but to venture a settlement upon unoffered lands, in the hope that the United States would not deal with *bona-fide* settlers so harshly as with mercenary speculators and land-jobbers. The settlers petitioned the Territorial or State Legislature for the right of purchasing land-holdings, and the Legislature memorialized the Congress in their behalf. The result was the grant of pre-emption.

The first general pre-emption act was passed May 29, 1830.[1] By this act every settler or occupant of the public lands, after giving due satisfaction and proof of settlement or improvement, was allowed to enter in the register of the Land Office any number of acres, up to a quarter section, at the established minimum price of $1.25 per acre. This act was to be in force only one year. It was not, therefore, a permanent system, but only a temporary measure.

This act, like any other of a similar character, was continued from year to year. The settlers petitioned Congress for its continuance on the ground of the incompleteness of survey, indistinctness of boundary-lines of settlement, or inaccessibility to district land offices. The act of June 22, 1838,[2] like previous acts, extended the right of pre-emption for two years, but it specified in detail the kinds of land to

---

[1] Statutes-at-Large, IV. 420-421.
[2] *Ibid.* V. 251-252.

which pre-emption could not be extended. The lands to which the Indian title was not yet extinguished; lands in any incorporated town; alternate sections of railroad and canal grants; lands for town-sites; reservations for educational purposes; and lands which had salt springs, were all exempted from the right of pre-emption. An act supplementary to this was passed on June 1, 1840, and extended the pre-emption right for another two years.[1]

It must be kept in mind that pre-emption was not yet a system. It still retained its temporary character. Successive legislative enactments kept it in force. Every act of pre-emption contemplated a relief to those settlers who occupied the lands before the passage of the act in question, but not to those who should settle after its passage. The ultimate effect of the measure was, however, the encouragement of unlawful occupation of the public lands. A measure to stop this became an indirect means of promoting it; for, in wild countries, pretext could easily be found and the title could easily be secured under the provisions of the pre-emption act. The law of pre-emption explicitly stipulates that its benefit is meant to be confined to actual settlers who were found on the public lands at the time of the passage of the act; and yet adventurous and unscrupulous men emigrated to the West and settled on unsurveyed public lands with the view of procuring another enactment and of extending pre-emption right.

Where population was scant and lands were plenty, but where there was a prospect of the future increase in value of landed property, the settlers could not be expected to await patiently the completion of a survey and the offering of land for sale, especially in case these settlers were foreign emigrants who went to the West with little knowledge of the topography of the country, and with little capital beyond their own labor and industry. It was very natural that such men

---

[1] Statutes-at-Large, V. 382.

should settle on the first piece of land which they found suited to agricultural purposes. Thus, the administration of land laws was made difficult, and some measures were found necessary to justify the title of the adventurous settlers. A remedy was found in the right of pre-emption. This was destined to become a permanent as well as a general system.

But was pre-emption an economic loss to the United States? So far as auction sales were concerned it was, but ultimately pre-emption proved a gain to the nation. What a new country needs is the actual improvement of its landed property, and when accomplished, such improvement redounds to the general prosperity of a State or nation.

The development of Western resources was the ultimate object of disposing of the public lands. Where settlers gathered together, and where improvements were made, there sprang up a new source of wealth. To scatter such a community because settlers trespassed on unoffered lands, would have been highly impolitic, especially at a time when the great West was still a wilderness or a desert.

Pre-emption was by no means a free grant. The pre-emptors had to pay the established price for their lands. To the United States the pre-emption grant amounted practically to the private sale of lands. The only sacrifice which the Government had to make was that of public sale, because the right of pre-emption closed the market to all other purchasers save actual settlers. The sacrifice of the public sale, however, was more than compensated by the improvement and settlement of the public lands. Webster was always friendly to the measure. In this view he sometimes differed from Clay.[1] The latter advocated that the law should be suffered to take its course, and that the unlawful improvements of settlers should be sold at public auction. But the two statesmen united in an effort to pass the general and permanent Pre-emption Act of 1841.[2]

---

[1] Webster's Works, IV. 398.
[2] Statutes-at-Large, V. 453.

CALHOUN'S OPPOSITION TO PRE–EMPTION.

From September 4, 1841, dates the permanent pre-emption right as a system of disposing of the public lands. The act was comprehensive, and the benefit of pre-emption extended to both native and foreign-born citizens. Mr. Calhoun figured as the stoutest opponent of pre-emption as well as of distribution measures, and advocated the cession of the public lands to the new States. He considered that the land laws of the United States could no longer be applied with advantage to the altered condition of the country, and, consequently, nothing but cession to the States could remedy the evils resulting from the public-land administration.

A brief quotation from one of his speeches will show his view of the public lands at this period. Calhoun said: "I regard the question of the public lands, next to that of the currency, the most dangerous and difficult of all which demand the attention of the country and the Government at this important juncture of our affairs." . . . . In offering the amendment I propose, I do not intend to controvert the justice of the eulogium which has been so often pronounced on our land system in the course of this discussion. On the contrary, I believe that it was admirably adjusted to effect its object when first adopted; but it must be borne in mind that a measure, to be perfect, must be adapted to circumstances, and that great changes have taken place in the lapse of fifty years since the adoption of the land system. At that time, the vast region now covered by the new States which have grown up on the public domain belonged to foreign powers, or was occupied by numerous Indian tribes, with the exception of a few sparse settlements on inconsiderable tracts, the Indian title to which was already at that time extinguished. Since then a mighty change has taken place. Nine States have sprung up as if by magic, with a population not less, probably, than two-fifths of the old States, and destined to surpass them in a few years in numbers, power and influence. That a change so mighty should so derange a system intended for an entirely different condition of things as to render important changes necessary to adapt it to present circumstances, is no more than might have been anticipated. .... ''Neither pre-emption nor distribution of the revenue received from the public lands can have any possible effect in correcting the disordered action of the system..... I have given to this question the most deliberate and careful examination, and have come to the conclusion that there is, and can be, no remedy short of cession—cession to the States respectively within which the lands are situated. The disease lies in ownership and administration, and nothing short of parting with both can reach it."[1] This was a dangerous and caustic remedy. Its failure saved the public lands, and preserved the best features in the present administration of the public domain.

The Pre-emption Act of 1841 gave right of preference to settlements on surveyed lands only, but later it was extended to unsurveyed lands in California, Oregon, Minnesota, Kansas, Nebraska, and New Mexico.[2] The right of preference was also extended to the alternate, even-numbered sections of the railroad grants, where the settlements were made prior to the withdrawal of these lands from the market.

PRESENT LAW OF PRE-EMPTION.[3]

The present law of pre-emption may be stated briefly as follows: Any person above the age of twenty-one years who is not the owner of 320 acres can enter the public lands, surveyed or unsurveyed, offered or unoffered. The essential requisites are actual residence and improvement. The maximum quantity of land allowed to any pre-emptor is 160 acres. For the final proof and payment, the period from

---

[1] Calhoun's Speeches, 403–404.
[2] Public Domain, 214.
[3] Revised Statutes, 414–419.

twelve to thirty-three months is allowed. The length of time for credit depends upon whether the land is offered or unoffered. Again, the price is at a minimum or double minimum, according to the situation of the land. If the land lies along the line of railroad grants, it is at double minimum; otherwise it is at a minimum. The benefit of pre-emption extends to foreign emigrants, upon filing a declaration of intention to become naturalized.

From the nature of pre-emption law, it can easily be seen that the pre-emption was an evolution from the two earlier methods of disposing of public lands—namely, credit sale and private contract. It is not a free grant, as we have already seen. It is a sale—a credit sale. It allows one almost three years to complete his title to a holding. The term is more liberal than under the credit system in former years, as it charges no interest. Again, the sale is private. It admits no competition. It is a private sale to specially favored settlers. The condition of contract is *bona-fide* settlement and actual cultivation. The essence of the contract differs in no respect from that which the Government made with the Ohio Company and Symmes' associates. As the Government granted a premium to these parties by selling them the lands at the reduced rate of two-thirds of a dollar, so now it does virtually the same thing for pre-emptors by excluding competition.

Thus pre-emption is a law of historical growth. But as it arose directly from the necessities of actual settlers, especially those of limited means, the dominant spirit of the law is actual residence and improvement. As such, it claims the title of the first American settlement law of a really beneficent character. The Public Land Commission say that " the pre-emption system was the result of law, experience, executive orders, departmental rulings and judicial construction. It has been many-phased, and was applied by special acts to special localities, with peculiar or additional features, but it has always contained, even to this day, the germ of actual settlement, under which thousands of homes have been made, and lands made productive, yielding a profit in crops to the farmer and increasing the resources of the nation."[1]

PRE-EMPTION NO LONGER NEEDED.

Changes in the land system since the passage of the Homestead Act introduced new features into pre-emption. The homestead law has eclipsed pre-emption, and pre-emption has now outlived its usefulness. The homestead law contains pre-emption features, and, in case a homesteader desires to avail himself of its provisions, facilities are given him to acquire title exactly on the same conditions as pre-emption. There seems now to be no necessity of retaining pre-emption as a system. On the contrary, it seems to be much abused by settlers. The same Public Land Commission which acknowledged the merit of pre-emption in its earlier years maintain that " the pre-emption laws are now the hope of the land-grabber, and are the land-swindler's darlings."[2] Mr. McFarland, the late Commissioner of the General Land Office, from time to time recommended Congress to repeal the pre-emption law. In his report for 1884, he says: " I renew previous recommendations for the repeal of the pre-emption law. . . . Economy of administration alone suggests such repeal, while the great abuses flowing from the illegal acquisition of land titles by fictitious pre-emption entries, and the exactions made upon *bona-fide* settlers, who are often obliged to buy off such claims in order to get access to public lands, render the repeal, in my judgment, a matter of public necessity."[3]

Lately, bills have been introduced into Congress which propose the repeal of the pre-emption law. No definite action has yet been taken upon them.[4] Mr. Sparks, the

---

[1] Public Domain, 215.

[2] *Ibid.* 678.

[3] Land Office Report, 1884, 6.

[4] See Public Domain, 679–682, and *Congressional Record*, January 7, 1884.

present Commissioner of the General Land Office, agreed with his predecessor in his opinion of pre-emption, and recommended its repeal in the Land Office Report for 1885. He says : " The pre-emption system no longer secures settlements by pre-emptors. If it did, or could be amended to do so, it would be useless for any good purpose, because supplanted by the more effective homestead law, if a home is the real object designed to be secured. If a home is not the object, the sooner the facility for obtaining land without making a home upon it which is offered by this system is removed from the statutes, the better for the settlement interests of the country and the future of its institutions."[1] Whether the Forty-Ninth Congress will repeal the law, remains to be seen.

Various Land Grants from 1841 to 1862.

During the period of twenty years in which the pre-emption law played the chief *rôle* in the land system, and served most efficiently the purpose for which it was enacted, several other important measures relating to the public lands were also passed, and some of them, like railroad grants and mining laws, are of such magnitude as to affect the economy of the whole country. It does not fall within the scope of this monograph to treat of railroad grants, much less of the mining laws. Readers are referred to special works on these subjects.[2]

We shall, however, briefly review a few of these important land measures.

---

[1] Land Office Report, 1885, 69–70.

[2] See article on Railroad Land Grants in *North American Review*, March, 1885, by J. W. Johnson. See also Our Public Land Policy, *Harper's Monthly*, October, 1885, by V. B. Paine; Railway Influence in the Land Office, *North American Review*, March, 1883, by George W. Julian ; and a rejoinder to the latter, The Railways and the U. S. Land Office, *Agricultural Review*, April, 1883, by Henry Beard.

For mining laws see Land Laws of Mining Districts, XII., Second Series J. H. U. Studies, by C. A. Shinn.

DONATION, SWAMP, AND GRADUATION ACTS.

Congress passed a donation act on August 4, 1842, for the Territory of East Florida.[1]   Persons who were able to bear arms, and to make actual settlements on certain sections of the Peninsula, were freely entitled to one-quarter section of land.   Another donation act was passed for Oregon Territory, September 27, 1850.   This granted to settlers public lands to the extent of from 160 to 640 acres, the quantity of land depending upon the priority of settlement and the domestic life of settlers.   If a settler was a married man, he was allowed from a half section to an entire section of land, one-half always being vested in the hands of his wife.   The donation act of Oregon Territory was followed by similar acts for the Territories of Washington and New Mexico, on March 2, 1853, and July 22, 1854 respectively.   Actual settlement and cultivation for four consecutive years were necessary to secure land grants under these donation acts.

These several donation acts were a premium upon settlement in the frontier sections of the country which were exposed to the attacks of Indians.   The settlements had, therefore, something of the character of military colonies of the ancient Republic, or of the Teutonic *Marches*.

These free grants of land were by no means a new feature in the land system of the United States.   They were inaugurated by the old Continental Congress.   Besides the grants of military, religious, and educational character, there were special grants to special individuals for certain meritorious services.   Precedents for special grants being numerous, the public lands were made subject to various schemes and projects not always of a laudable character.   The inauguration of such settlement laws as pre-emption checked many schemes.

In 1849,[2] Congress inaugurated a system that led to the grant of immense areas of swamps and overflowed lands to

---

[1] Statutes-at-Large, V. 502–504.

[2] *Ibid.* IX. 352.

the States in which such areas are situated. In the following year, Illinois had the first railroad land grant, which was followed by a series of grants to various railroad corporations.

In 1854, the Graduation Act was passed. This was to cheapen, for the benefit of actual settlers and for adjoining farms, the price of lands which had been long in the market.

EARLY MOVEMENT FOR HOMESTEADS.

We now come to the Homestead Act, the most important of all the settlement laws. The movement to secure homesteads to actual settlers may be traced as far back as 1833, when Evans began to agitate his land reform through a paper called *The Radicals.* It was a movement against land monopoly which was destined soon to become an anti-slavery measure. Mr. Webster, in his speech on the Graduation Bill in 1839, said: " As to donation to actual settlers, I have often expressed the opinion, and still entertain it, that it would have been a wise policy of Government from the first to make a donation of a half or whole quarter section to every actual settler, the head of a family, upon condition of habitation and cultivation; that this would have been far better and freer from abuse than any system of pre-emption."[1] This speech represented a general policy which was advocated by the Whigs against retrocession. To oppose cession to the States was to oppose the propagation of slavery, for, if the new States should receive public lands as advocated by the representatives of slave-holding States, they would eventually come into servile ways of thinking and would be lost to free States.

AGITATION BY " FREE-SOILERS."

In 1844, Evans advocated, in the *People's Rights*, the following points: (1) Freedom of the public lands in a limited quantity to actual settlers; (2) Cessation of the sale

---

[1] Webster's Works, IV. 525.

of public lands to non-resident purchasers; (3) The exemption of homesteads, and (4) The restriction of the purchase of any other land to a limited quantity.[1] This was the year in which President Polk was elected. In four years from that time, land agitation had become a potent factor in American politics. A party called "Free-Soil Democracy" now appeared. This party consisted of two elements, political Free-Soilers and conscientious Free-Soilers. The former were confined to the State of New York, and were called "Night-Soilers" by an opposing party. The latter were found in every Northern State; scattered also through Delaware, Maryland, Virginia, and Kentucky. The conscientious Free-Soilers were frequently called "Abolitionists."

In 1848, the Free-Soil Democracy held a National Convention at Buffalo, and nominated John P. Hale, of New Hampshire, for President, and Charles F. Adams, of Massachusetts, for Vice-President. The Free-Soilers seceded from the Democrats, but did not join the Whigs. They determined to secure free soil for a free people, and to restrict slavery to its State limits. They said that "Congress had no more power to make a slave than to make a king." So they refused to introduce slavery into new Territories. In the Thirty-First Congress, the Free-Soilers were represented by only two Senators and only fourteen Representatives. In the Thirty-Second Congress, the Senators increased in number to three, and the Congressmen to seventeen. Charles Sumner was then a Free-Soil Senator.[2]

In the Presidential year of 1852, the Free-Soil Democracy held a National Convention at Pittsburg, and nominated John P. Hale, of New Hampshire, and George W. Julian, of Indiana, for President and Vice-President respectively. They inserted the following clause in their platform: "That the public lands of the United States belong to the people,

---

[1] Meyer's Heimstätten und andere Wirthschaftsgesetze, 403.

[2] See Free-Soil Party, by Alexander Johnston, in Cyclopædia of Political Science.

and should not be sold to individuals, nor granted to corporations, but should be held as a sacred trust for the benefit of the people, and should be granted in limited quantities, free of cost, to landless settlers." Thus the free-soil or homestead movement became a national question.

Mr. Seward was then advocating in the Senate a homestead law. In his speech on the public domain which was delivered in the Senate February 27, 1851, he said: "The gratuitous distribution of public lands to actual settlers is marked by equal humanity and good sense." Again, he said: "All will admit—all do admit—that the power over the domain should be so exercised as to favor the increase of population, the augmentation of wealth, the cultivation of virtue, and the diffusion of happiness." He further argued, from the point of industry, that "the first and fundamental interest of the Republic is the cultivation of its soil. That cultivation is the sole fountain of the capital or wealth which supplies every channel of industry."[1]

In the Presidential year of 1856, there arose the new Republican party, which grew out of the Free-Soil Democracy and the Whigs. From that time no more was heard of the Free-Soil party, but its principles were represented in the platform of the new party. Free homes and the restriction of slavery were the main issues of the Republicans, as previously of the Free-Soil Democracy.

HOMESTEAD BILLS IN CONGRESS.

In 1859, the struggle for a homestead law began in Congress. The bill passed the House of Representatives by a majority vote of 120 to 76; but it failed in the Senate. It was the Cuban bill that obstructed the passage of the Homestead Act. The two bills were of opposing character, one pro-slavery, and the other for free soil. On this point Mr. Seward said in the Senate: "After nine hours' yielding to the

---

[1] Seward's Works, I. 156–162.

discussion of the Cuban question, it is time to come back to the great question of the day and the age. The Senate may as well meet face to face the issue which is before them. It is an issue presented by the competition between the two questions. One, the homestead bill, is a question of homes, of lands for the landless freemen of the United States. The Cuba bill is the question of slaves for the slave-holders of the United States."[1]

Although the friends of the Homestead Act did not then succeed in passing it, yet it was destined to come up again, and that soon. The following year Mr. Grow, of Pennsylvania, introduced the bill in the House. On March 12, it passed the House and went to the Senate. In the Senate, however, Mr. Johnson's substitute for the House bill was adopted, and this, after a protracted conference with the House, was finally accepted. Mr. Johnson's bill differed from the original House bill in not allowing pre-emptors to enjoy the benefit of the homestead law. The Senate bill also confined its provisions to lands which were subject to private entry. It limited the minimum age of settlers to twenty-five years. There were also some other differences in the Senate bill as distinguished from that of the House. Suffice it to say, through the efforts of the members of the House Committee, a compromise was effected, and much of a restrictive character in the Senate bill gave way to the more liberal elements of the House bill. The compromise was by no means satisfactory, even to the members of the committee, but it was the best they could obtain from the Senate. On this point, Mr. Colfax, a member of the Conference Committee, said to the House: "We regard this as but a single step in advance toward a law, which we shall demand from the American Congress, enacting a comprehensive and liberal homestead policy. This we have agreed to as merely *avant-courier*."[2] Mr. Grow also said that they agreed with the

---

[1] Seward's Works, IV. 59.
[2] Public Domain, 339.

Senate bill on the principle of "half a loaf is better than no bread."

President Buchanan's Veto.[1]

The compromise bill passed both Houses of Congress by a large majority; but on June 23, President Buchanan vetoed the bill and returned it to the Senate. The first objection of Buchanan was based on constitutional grounds. The veto-message dwelt particularly on this point, and urged that Congress had no power to give away public lands either to individuals or to States. This was an old objection which had been raised against the policy of internal improvement by its opponents. There were too many precedents in the way of Buchanan's constitutional objection. A second objection was partiality. The message urged: "It will prove unequal and unjust in its operation among the actual settlers themselves." The point was that if the new-comers were allowed to acquire land free or at the insignificant price of twenty-five cents per acre, the old-comers would suffer from the reduction of the price of their real estate. The same objection was raised also in behalf of old soldiers who received Government lands for their services in the Army. Again, the homestead law was unjust because it favored only one class of people—namely, the agricultural class—at the expense of other avocations. It was unjust, moreover, to the older States of the Union, because, first, it would deprive them of their just proportion of the public revenue; and, second, it would deprive them of population through the encouragement of free farms. A third objection was that the homestead law would open a vast field for speculation. Buchanan was afraid that homesteaders would become the mere tools of capitalists. His fourth objection was that the law did not extend the same privileges to native and naturalized citizens. The latter, though not heads of families, were assured of a free farm, while the former had to be masters of

---

[1] For the text, see Public Domain, 342–345.

households in order to secure the benefits of the law. A fifth objection was that partiality would be shown among the pre-emptors themselves. The existing pre-emptors could secure the lands at the reduced price of 62½ cents per acre, but future pre-emptors would have to pay the full minimum price. The sixth and last objection was that the homestead law would deprive the Government of a source of public revenue. The message said the bill "lays the ax at the root of our present admirable land system." In conclusion, the message declared: "The people of the United States have advanced with steady but rapid strides to their present condition of power and prosperity. They have been guided in their progress by the fixed principle of protecting the equal rights of all, whether they be rich or poor. No agrarian sentiment has ever prevailed among them. The honest poor man by frugality and industry can, in any part of our country, acquire a competence for himself and his family, and in doing this he feels that he eats the bread of independence. He desires no charity, either from the Government or from his neighbors. This bill, which proposes to give him land at an almost nominal price out of the property of the Government, will go far to demoralize the people and repress this noble spirit of independence."

The veto thus unfortunately deprived the Democratic party of the honor and merit of passing the homestead bill. The two great parties kept their party lines with regard to the public land. It was the Democratic party that secured the acquisitions, and it was the Republican party that passed most of the settlement laws. Each party has done its peculiar service to the country.

FINAL PASSAGE OF THE HOMESTEAD ACT.

On July 8, 1861, a homestead bill was introduced in the House of Representatives. The bill received the immediate attention of the whole House, and after being referred successively to the Committee on Agriculture and to the Committee on Public Lands, it passed the House on February 28, 1862. About a month later the House bill was taken up by the Senate. As in the previous session of Congress, a substitute for the whole bill was introduced by a Senator from Virginia, but this time it failed to be carried. After a few amendments, the House bill passed the Senate by a vote of thirty-three to seven. Agreements were soon effected with the House, and the bill received the approval of President Lincoln on May 20, 1862.

This original homestead law has been amended several times, and each amendment has granted more liberal provisions to actual settlers. But the fundamental principle of the Homestead Act is the grant of a free homestead to *bona-fide* settlers. This principle has never been lost from view.

The homestead law,[1] as it now stands, grants to every applicant who is the head of a family or above the age of twenty-one, one hundred and sixty acres of public land or a less quantity in legal subdivisions, free of charge, except certain fees to the Register, on the condition of actual settlement and cultivation. The title passes to the homesteader after five years' residence upon the holding. But if he desires to secure the title earlier, he can do so by paying the Government the full minimum price of the land. This is known as "the commutation of homestead entries," and it virtually comes under the provisions of the pre-emption act. In the same way a pre-emptor can change to a homestead entry. Thus the homestead law embraces the pre-emption provision, while pre-emption is limited to only one form of acquiring the title—that is, to a legalized private purchase at the minimum price of unoffered land. Since this is secured through a homestead provision, the uselessness of the pre-emption law is apparent, except as it enables settlers to avail themselves of the two acts, and thus increase the size of their holdings to three hundred and twenty acres.

---

[1] Revised Statutes, 419–424.

↣ The most beneficial provision of the act is the exemption of the homestead from the obligation of debt contracted prior to the issue of the patent. This enables a settler to build up a new homestead free from any embarrassment under which he might have labored previous to his settlement. After the patent passes to the settler, he is protected by the homestead-exemption law of the State in which it lies. ↄ

Besides the homestead provision to ordinary settlers, there are so-called Soldiers' Homesteads and Indian Homesteads. The former extends the benefits of the homestead law to those who served in the Army or Navy during the late Civil War. The length of time the soldier was in the Army is deducted from the term of five years, or, in other words, the service in the Army is considered as a substitute for actual residence. Indian homesteads are granted to those Indians who have abandoned their tribal relations. These homesteads are inalienable for the period of five years after the issue of the patent.

EULOGIES OF THE HOMESTEAD LAW.

Many eulogies have been pronounced upon the homestead law, some of which may well be cited here. The Public Land Commission say: "The Homestead Act is now the approved and preferred method of acquiring title to the public lands, ... and was the outgrowth of a system extending through nearly eighty years, and now, within the circle of a hundred years since the United States acquired the first of her public lands, the Homestead Act stands as the concentrated wisdom of legislation for settlement of the public lands. It protects the Government, it fills the States with homes, it builds up communities, and lessens the chances of social and civil disorder by giving ownership of the soil, in small tracts, to the occupants thereof. It was copied from no other nation's system. It was originally and distinctly American, and remains a monument to its originators."

A land lawyer of repute, in Washington, Mr. Copp, says:[1] "To the people of Europe, where the high price of real estate confers distinction upon its owner, it seems beyond belief that the United States should give away one hundred and sixty acres of land for nothing. Yet such is the fact; a compliance with the homestead law, and the payment of small fees and commissions to the local officers, secure title to a quarter section of Government land. Laborers in other countries, who find it difficult to support their families, can here acquire wealth, social privileges and political honors by a few years of intelligent industry and patient frugality. All in the Atlantic States who are discouraged with the slow, tedious methods of reaching independence, will find rich rewards awaiting settlers on the public lands who have talent and energy, while the unfortunate in business, and they who are burdened with debt can, in the West and South, start anew in the race of life, for the homestead law expressly declares that 'no lands acquired under the provisions of this chapter (Homestead) shall in any event become liable to the satisfaction of any debt contracted prior to the issuing of the patent therefor.'"

The value of the homestead law for opening the Western country cannot be over-estimated. It will remain as *the* land law of the United States as long as the public lands continue to exist.

THE EDUCATIONAL LAND GRANTS.

Soon after the passage of the homestead law, Congress granted to all the States 30,000 acres of land for each Representative and Senator in Congress, for the purpose of establishing agricultural and mechanical institutions. Historically, this was an outgrowth of the early educational land grants for common schools and seminaries.[2]

---

[1] The American Settler's Guide, 25.

[2] Federal Land Grants for Education in the Northwest Territory, by Dr. Geo. W. Knight, Papers of American Historical Association, I., No. 3.

TIMBER AND DESERT LAND ACTS.

Acts which relate more directly to the settlers in the West are the Timber Culture and Desert Land Acts. The former was passed on March 3, 1873,[1] and grants to settlers treeless lands to the extent of 160 acres for the encouragement of tree culture. While certain sections of the public lands were treeless, and thus needed the donation of lands for tree culture, other sections are chiefly valuable for timber and stone. These are chiefly on the Pacific Coast. An act was passed June 3, 1878,[2] authorizing the sale of timber and stone lands to the extent of 160 acres each, at $2.50 per acre. At the same time a strict law was enacted for the prevention of timber depredations on the public lands. The Desert Land Act was passed on March 3, 1877.[3] This allows, on a credit for three years, an entry of 640 acres of desert land—that is, land which does not produce agricultural crops without irrigation. Both the Timber and Desert Land Acts have been repeatedly condemned as a source of fraudulent entries, and their repeal has been recommended by the late Commissioner of the General Land Office.

CONCLUSION.

In conclusion, we shall recapitulate a few important points. All the public lands of the United States, except those reserved for special purposes, are sold at public sale and by private entry. They are classified as follows: 1. Mineral lands; 2. Timber and stone lands; 3. Saline lands; 4. Townsite lands; 5. Desert lands; 6. Coal lands; and 7. Agricultural lands. They are disposed of under special laws governing each class. The agricultural lands are subject to the settlement laws—namely, pre-emption and homestead.

---

[1] Statutes-at-Large, XVII. 605–606.
[2] *Ibid*. XX. 89.
[3] *Ibid*. XIX. 377.

But, as soon as surveys are completed, they are offered also
at public sale, in which the highest bidder can purchase any
amount of land.   After a public sale the remaining lands are
allowed for private entry.   Through various kinds of sales,
grants, and settlements, the public lands have been rapidly
disposed of.   The available lands of various descriptions,
exclusive of Alaska, which still remain unsold amount to
more than six hundred and forty million acres.   This is
more by twenty million acres than all the lands hitherto
disposed of since the acquisition of the public lands down to
1883.   The nation's interest truly demands wise, economic,
and judicious administration of the remaining public
property.   But this is impossible without first reforming
the existing land laws, which are much abused by unscrupulous land grabbers.   Again, during the interval between
1850 and 1872, an enormous amount of lands had been
granted to railroad corporations.   The grants amounted to
more than one hundred and fifty-five million acres.   Of these,
more than one-third had already been patented, but the rest
ought to be recovered by the Government on account of non-
fulfillment of various conditions stipulated in the grants, as
well as for the interest of honest settlers.   Commissioner
Sparks says of these unpatented lands: "The amount of
unpatented lands embraced in all the grants subject to declaration of forfeiture is estimated at one hundred million acres,
an area equal to that of the combined States of New York,
New Jersey, Pennsylvania, Delaware, Maryland and Virginia.   The restoration to public settlement and entry of
this great body of lands is a subject of the first magnitude
and of profound national importance.   The question presented
is strictly one of legal right.   The default of the companies
has been voluntary.   The rights of the public are now to be
considered—the right of the people to repossess themselves
of their own.   The case is not one calling for sympathy to
the corporations: it is one calling for justice to the people."[1]

---

[1] Land Office Report, 1885, 44.

Public opinion inclines to agree with Commissioner Sparks. Although the public domain is of such vast extent, and the laws pertaining to it are so complex that some persons think that there are too many obstructions in the way of honest administration of the land laws—such obstructions, for example, as land grabbers and cattle kings—to my mind the present question of land administration in the United States is perfectly simple. Indeed, two words would suffice to indicate clearly the future policy of the public-land administration. These words are REFORM and RECOVERY—*reform of legal abuses and recovery of the public lands from railroad corporations.*